KALEIDOSCOPE

DEVON

Edited by Michelle Warrington

First published in Great Britain in 1999 by
POETRY NOW YOUNG WRITERS
Remus House,
Coltsfoot Drive,
Woodston,
Peterborough, PE2 9JX
Telephone (01733) 890066

Copyright Contributors 1999

HB ISBN 0 75431 444 8
SB ISBN 0 75431 445 6

FOREWORD

This year, the Poetry Now Young Writers'
Kaleidoscope competition proudly presents the best
poetic contributions from over 32,000 up-and-coming
writers nationwide.

Successful in continuing our aim of promoting
writing and creativity in children, each regional
anthology displays the inventive and original writing
talents of 11-18 year old poets. Imaginative,
thoughtful, often humorous, *Kaleidoscope Devon*
provides a captivating insight into the issues and
opinions important to today's young generation.

The task of editing inevitably proved challenging, but
was nevertheless enjoyable thanks to the quality of
entries received. The thought, effort and hard work
put into each poem impressed and inspired us all. We
hope you are as pleased as we are with the final result
and that you continue to enjoy *Kaleidoscope Devon*
for years to come.

CONTENTS

Exeter School

Robert Horton	56
Lee Palmer	57
Matthew Tyrer	58
Robert Grieg-Gran	59
Damien Mansell	60
Fabien Flight	60
Chris Horne	61

Great Torrington School

Cara Horrell	61
Jessica May	62
Sarah Ford	62
Paul Elkins	63
Riki Johnson	63
Darren Redford	64
Robert Lee	64
Sarah Heywood	65
Francine Downton	65
Gemma Robinson	66
Lewis Parker	66
Ross Mitchell	67
James Pyke	67
Jamie Thompson	68
Susie Williams	68
Claire Ashton	69
Helen Laney	69
Nicky Hymas	70
James Mathews	71
Cleo Bott	71
Karla Bissett	72
Timothy Brush	72
Charlene Potts	73
Jack Elliott	73
Zoey Cook	74
Jenny Preece	74
Lisa Mitchell	75
Natalie Oliver	76
Claire Harriss	76

Anne-Marie Redford	77
Holly Clerc-De-Saux	77
Sarah Mills	78
Michelle Ellis	78
Grace Hicks	79
Ben Jackson	80
Bryony Maycock	81
John Woollacott	82
Sarah Beer	82
Tarnya Davies	83
Thomas Blight	84
Claire Whitehouse	84
Samantha Paine	85
Harriet Toogood	85
Alice Brosnan-Guers	86
Keith Bateman	86
Nicholas Hunt	87
Amy Anderson	87
Benjamin Smart	88
Dawn Ryan	88
Josh Catling	89
Gina Hocking	90
Leitza Gorman	90
Jay Whiting	91
Amy Boyd	91
Andrew J Robinson	92
Robin Judson	92
Katie Elston	93
Alex Brine	93
Jenny Le-Seelleur	94
Sarah Ashton	95
Karis Craven-Wilkinson	95
Kate Clements	96
Nicholas Bale	96
Tom Williams	97
Katy Greenslade	97
Debbie Elkins	98
Samantha Headon	98

Chloë Threadgould	99
Dale Partridge	99
Jessica Day	100
Vicky Anderson	100
Ian Gilbert	101
Emma Heywood	101
Oliver Lulham	102
Kerry Vanstone	102
Lucy Kesseler	102
Edward Haskins	103
Andrea Reed	103
Sarah Jennings	104
Ian Gilbert	104
Kyla Manenti	105
Lee K Holmes	105
Ralph Atton	106
Carly-Jo Daniels	106
Michael Day	107
Louise Bond	107
Matthew Grainger	108
James Norris	108
Louise Headon	109
Hannah Stanley	109
Tannaze Tinati	110
Rachel Knight	111
Abigail Worth	111
Lance Appleton	111
Kyle Warrington	112
Lisa Harper	112
Lee Cockwill	113
Karl Curtis	113
Ben Jenkinson	114
Jamie Ellis	114
Adam Vanstone	115
Dane Jenkins	115
Matthew A Phillips	116
Tim Judson	117
Felicity Reid	117

The Poems

WHIRLING SEASONS

Awaken to the dawn of day,
Stretching to the start of May,
The buds are sprouting in the green,
With dots of colour in-between.
The birds are chirping in the trees,
Adorned with busy, buzzing bees.
A drop of dew lies at my feet,
And in the soil, snowdrops meet.
At lunchtime as I eat a treat,
Summer comes with scorching heat.
Colours all are burning bright,
Amidst a ray of hazy light.
And all of noon is oh so boiling,
Sunburn all the day is spoiling.
All the buds are brightly glowing,
Summer now is clearly showing.
I often miss these precious hours,
Dozing off amongst the flowers,
For now's the time for lemonade,
And reading comics in the shade.
Then off the oak tree falls a leaf,
And autumn now will show his teeth.
Fruit with quite a touch of taste,
Never ever's made to waste.
Harvest time is at last here,
This is the time the fields to clear.
For in our houses is the corn,
Wherein a loaf of bread is born.
And in the trees there's not a bird,
For they have gone without a word.
And all the leaves they drop and fall
Over the next-door neighbour's wall.
The colour is a rainy brown,
When stormy days are spent from town.

Then when the wind begins to nip,
And on the ice we slide and slip,
The evening now has left and gone,
The cold's come back to everyone.
And snowflakes drift to the muddy ground,
Then float away without a sound.
But then (oh wow!) it's nearly here,
Spicing up winter with Christmas cheer,
Opening up a Christmas wish,
An hour nobody should miss.
Then off to a warm and blanketed bed,
With heavy eyes and a weary head,
Ready to start another day,
With seasons flashing all away.

Rachel Smith *(11)*

A NEW DAWN

The Roundheads slashed the weary Cavaliers
Black death destroyed the land
Invasion by the Napoleonic plague
Weeping widows wondering what might have been
Bombs dropping, fire spreading
Anthill had seen it all.

A child dozed on the flowerless common
The devil of winter had died
The eagle of summer flew down spreading new life
He perched upon a tree, his menacing eyes piercing my imagination
Oh, so gold was he, he was the Lord of summer not known to me.
Anthill had seen it all.

He swooped down and won my heart.
A blazing flame he squawked and cooed above the trees so high
He flew down, no flowers there
Behind his gaping figure a tiny poppy stood
The beauty hit my eyes, I gasped
Is this all it had to show for the plunderous evil placed here
                                      throughout history?
Anthill had seen it all.

Sam Farley (11)
Devonport High School For Boys

DREAM

A picture in a swirling mist,
Bright colours all around,
Like petals off a wilting flower,
Floating softly to the ground.
A ray of light shines through the clouds,
On a princess young and fair,
Her lips like a red, red rose,
And golden, glowing hair.
A melody hangs on the breeze,
Enchanting like her eyes,
While bluebirds fly up heavenwards,
Through the sapphire skies.
Suddenly, there, through the mist,
A building standing tall,
Within a moment everything stops,
There is no sound at all.
Then, the silence breaks!
And out the castle comes,
A great big dragon breathing fire,
So everybody runs.
The dragon breathes and lets out fire,
The pretty flowers it burns,
He kills the birds and princess fair,
And then to me he turns . . .

Suddenly I wake up sharp,
My bedside lamp switched on,
But the memory of that dream,
Is thankfully now gone!

Sophie Perks (12)
Edgehill College

4

NIGHTMARES

She raced through the wilderness
As she heard the clock chime.
She stopped, stared, full of horror
In that land of frozen time.

Massive spiders with evil eyes
Approached from land and seas and skies
And stroked their legs across her thighs.

She turned. Her house was covered in flames!
She screamed and screamed, but no sound came.

She raced around
But only terror could find
In the crooked circles
Of her frightened mind.

Rebecca Taylor (12)
Edgehill College

THE BARN OWL

The barn owl glides in the breeze,
Its eyes are never at ease.
It swoops down to catch its prey,
On it its talons squeeze,
And then quickly flies away.
They squeak and squawk at the tip of their tongue,
All of it shared between its hungry young,
And then there is sheer silence as they wait,
Only to hear the whine of the farmer's gate.

Ruth Verney (12)
Edgehill College

MY BUDGIE

We were very surprised,
When my budgie Emma died,
Our other budgie George,
Was all alone.
Without his little mate he was getting in a state,
So we brought another budgie home.
My new budgie is called Annie,
She is very, very canny.
She managed to get out of the cage,
By head-butting the door with rage!
She flies around with George,
Every other day and night.
She eats and eats and eats,
Then sits on the curtain rod,
And tweets and tweets and tweets!
My budgie Annie does strange things,
She shrieks and shrieks,
Until your ears ring!

Catherine Jennings (12)
Edgehill College

I WISH I HAD A PUPPY

I wish I had a puppy,
to walk with every day,
I do not want a guppy,
as they don't come out to play.

I'd feed him in the morning,
and then again at night,
I'd teach him to be gentle,
and never ever bite.

I'd like a pet to play with,
a dog would be just fine,
I'd be prepared to share him,
but he always would be mine.

Anna Hornblow (12)
Edgehill College

THE TARKA TRAIL

I wish I was on the Tarka Trail,
On my mountain bike,
Not stuck in doing my homework
That's what I really like!

I want to feel the wind in my hair,
And the sunshine on my face,
Not shut up inside my bedroom
I want to be in the open space!

I really need some exercise,
To keep myself fit,
I feel like my hammy in her cage,
Please let me out for a bit!

My friends have gone out there,
Wheels buzzing away like bees,
Then they stop for a picnic
And run around the trees!

It's brilliant on the BMX track,
Like a roller-coaster bumpy and fast,
I hope I don't fall off, but I'm happy
Because I've finished this poem at last!

April Castle (11)
Edgehill College

THE WORLD THROUGH AN UGLY KALEIDOSCOPE

The trees are bare; the flowers are dead,
The air is thick with smoke and pollution.
Rubbish litters the streets and alleys,
The houses are nothing but pathetic piles of rubble.

The rainforests are gone, demolished and dead,
The last wild animals have died in zoos.
The friendly morning chorus disappeared years ago,
All the birds went with it, too.

The seas are great swamps of mud and gunge,
The fishes lie dead washed up on the shore.
Old beach houses lie devastated, in ruins,
With not even a long gone memory of happiness remaining.

The once proud and gleaming cities,
Are now reduced to worthless piles of stone.
The remainders of fast foreign cars lie destroyed and rusting
                                                    on the roads
With street lamps lying across them, dark and decaying.

The last of the human race wander the streets struggling to survive,
Attempting to find any last scrap of food;
They scan the streets for a drink, crumb or dead human to quench
                                                    their hunger,
Disappointed at every vain attempt.

The warmth of human love has vanished,
Every last bit of happiness is gone and deceased.
No more lovers walking the streets, hand in hand,
No more happy families, laughing and contented,
Not even one long gone trace of a happy memory.

The world through an ugly kaleidoscope,
A terrifying thought,
But is this just a horrible fiction
Or is this the future the world deserves?

Moira Johns (11)
Edgehill College

SHADOWS OF THE NIGHT

The shadows seemed to disappear into an endless forest of darkness.
There was a never-ending tunnel of gloom, that seemed to be reaching
out to me,
Wrapping its ice-cold hands around me,
Urging me to go on,
Through the ripping claws of thorn bushes that hung in the gentle,
chilled breeze.

The mist and fog clouded my mind and I was left in a daze.
But still I kept on forcing my way through the darkness.
Then suddenly my mind ran riot,
Figures from the deepest, darkest part of my mind
Appeared in front of me and blurred my vision.

I could hear the quiet whispering of the trees and the gentle howl
of the wind.
The bat-like figures flew past me tearing my skin.
I lay down like a wilted rose in a garden of thorns,
When all of a sudden the wind died,
Darkness was restored to light:
Up above me I saw the clouds part,
Then beams of light stood around me.

Sadie England (13)
Edgehill College

WAR

Blurred shapes shoot past,
As doom flies past.
Men cry in pain,
This war is no game.
Falling bodies everywhere,
Enemy and foe all aglare.
Blood oozing onto the ground,
Bang! Gunshots all around.
Cannons roaring,
Missiles soaring,
Water-logged trenches,
The air filled with stench.
Captains ordering,
Friends mourning.
All is gloom,
Mankind is doomed.

Rebecca Slade (11)
Edgehill College

FLUFFY

Two pointy ears,
A pink wet nose,
Black silky body,
Who knows?
         - It's Fluffy.

Cuddles up tight,
Furry white toes,
Never starts a fight,
Who knows?
         - It's Fluffy.

Big green eyes,
A baby in his paws,
He miaows, never cries,
Who knows?
    - It's Fluffy.
My adorable, snuggly cat.

Amani Omejer (11)
Edgehill College

TRISTAMENTE

I sit on the smooth seat
And its polished surface seems to encourage me,
As I move into a dream
Of wild scenes and summer days.

I lovingly finger the soft white keys
As I close my eyes and imagine,
I search the maze of my mind
To try and decide which tune to play.

Shall I play what's in my head?
Shall I play what's in my heart?
I know!

My head is filled with this one song;
A sad song - a sad song.
The piano feels my sorrow,
And the tune slips out of my fingers.

It strays over the ghostly whiteness,
And falls like teardrops from the waiting strings.
Floating around the room it gradually slows,
Flower, softer, slower, stop.

Jennifer Dare (13)
Edgehill College

A Poem

My cats are tall, my cats are sleek,
My cats are sneaky Siamese,
They're sleek and cunning, they're very sweet.
Bertie is a little fat,
Fergus is a shy old thing.
In the night they cry and moan,
In the morning they call and groan.
Across the fields and through the door,
To the cellar for their food,
Like a pack of hungry wolves,
They eat and eat until they're full.
The morning has gone, noon has come,
Now it's time for their evening run.
The day is over, it's time for grub,
So across the fields and a scratch at the door.
Here come the hungry pack of wolves.

Lucy Govan (11)
Edgehill College

Racehorse

Bang! And we're off.
The race has begun,
The going is soft,
Just like the sun:

Not too hot, not too cold.
My heart is now racing,
I'm feeling so bold,
But must hold back, start pacing.

I've turned the last bend,
The end is in sight.
I've jumped the last fence,
Must take my flight.

I'm ahead by a length
And gasping for air.
Guess what? I've won!
Not bad for an old grey mare.

Anneka Ranken (11)
Edgehill College

THE UNCARING WORLD

T ears in the eyes of the hungry - the world doesn't care.
H ungry children with no hope at all - the world doesn't care.
E njoyment, excitement - the world cares.

U nimaginable sorrow - the world doesn't care.
N owhere to sleep at night - the world doesn't care.
C arbon dioxide ruining the atmosphere - the world doesn't care.
A nimals getting killed for human materials - the world doesn't care.
R ainforests destroyed for building on - the world doesn't care.
I ndustry destroying all natural beauty - the world doesn't care.
N ot enough fossil fuels left - the world doesn't care.
G ame shows, winning thousands - the world cares.

W andering travellers seeking rest and refuge - the world doesn't care.
O il being dumped in the sea - the world doesn't care.
R eally sick people - the world doesn't care.
L onely people with no friends at all - the world doesn't care.
D o we *ever* think of *anyone* but ourselves?

Chris Patt (13)
Edgehill College

GOD REACHED DOWN

God reached down, breathed on Earth,
The world unfolded, came alive!
Then of course mankind arrived.

'Not bad,' they said.
'A good beginning, but in need
Of just one or two small improvements.'

A few years on and what have we got?
A *lot!*
Hacksaws hacking,
Factories polluting,
Rainforests and clean air
Have been taken off God's top ten,
But who cares? 'Spend, spend, *spend!*'
Is the new chart topper!

Nature is disappearing
Beneath the revolting air,
The Earth is leaving,
And soon it will be bare.

So stop the hacksaws hacking,
Stop the polluters polluting,
Because soon it will be too late.

Olivia Bargery (10)
Edgehill College

THEY NEVER LIKED MY CAT ...

I walked around our cramped little house,
Wandering from room to room,
Into the kitchen that's being refitted,
The shelf that she used to sit on,
Her food bowl in the bin,
Like she never existed.
They never liked my cat,
But the kitchen room feels empty without her.

Into the colourful living room,
Decorated in Mum's awful taste,
The new three piece suite in the corner;
They never let her sit on that chair,
Too many hairs they said.
They never liked my cat,
But the living room feels empty without her.

Into the dining room I go,
Where she had her own special chair.
It's been taken away now,
Broken up for its wood;
Shows how much they thought of her.
They never liked my cat,
But the dining room feels empty without her.

I'll never forget her gentle purr,
The elegant way she walked.
She was considered a bother,
A nothing on four legs.
They never liked my cat,
But the house will always feel empty without her.

Pandora Garwood (13)
Edgehill College

MY BROTHER

My brother is very tall,
And he thinks he is so cool.
Everyone with him thinks he's wrong,
As he lazes about all day long.

He screams all the time to Mum and Dad,
Because they always accuse him of being bad.
To me he is hardly ever kind,
But despite this I don't really mind.

Sadly, girls really like him;
To be honest though I don't really blame them.
He is quite nice to girls his age,
To stay away from them he needs to be locked in a cage.

But brother will be brothers,
Like sisters will be sisters.
Despite what I said he can be good,
And anyway I'm just as bad.

Isabel Heming (10)
Edgehill College

MY BIG BROTHER

My big brother is such a pain!
Although people say they're all the same.
Doesn't do homework, doesn't like school,
All he's interested in is playing pool.

He's never very tidy,
He's never very clean,
His bedroom is a mess
And hardly can be seen.

My brother's never really home,
He's always with his mate;
My mum gets really mad with him
Especially when he's late.

My dad can always see
The funny side of him
And tells my mum to let him go
Because, he's not that bad
You know!

Lisa Baker (11)
Edgehill College

HIGH TIDE

As the waves crashed
on the rocks,
the tide rose higher and
higher.
The wind howled as if
in temper,
ever growing louder and
stronger.
The sky grew darker,
the only light
was the flicker of a
lighthouse.

The wind became silent,
the sea went calm,
the waves drifted
away
and left a deserted
beach.

Rebecca Heard (13)
Edgehill College

STEAM FAIR DAY

The gears are whirring,
The coal fire's burning.
Driver with his oily cap,
Hands and face also black.
Pressure in the boiler rising,
Belt and flywheel quickly striding.
The lights thereon shining brightly,
Brass and paintwork polished nightly.

The people come from near and far,
By train, by plane but mostly car.
All the exhibits there to see,
Small and large for you and me.
Fairground music sounding loud,
Take a ride fast and proud;
The Wall of Death amazing all,
The crowd waiting to see them fall.

Showman's engines in a row,
Engines thudding and lights aglow.
From the stage the show goes on,
Balloons, streamers and sounds of song.
Engines whistle their applause,
The singers have to take a pause.
Land of Hope and Glory sung,
Steam fair day is nearly done.

The Showman's hymn and Auld Lang Syne,
We say farewell just one more time.

James Littlejohns (13)
Edgehill College

I DIDN'T TOUCH A DROP, UNLUCKILY SOMEONE DID!

Tears flooded their eyes,
Fingers went numb,
Bodies shook;
Did he see it come?

He didn't handle a bottle,
Not even a drop,
Others did;
But they didn't stop.

He tried to walk home,
It was getting late;
He was fine,
Until he reached his fate.

A skid of the shiny machine,
Crash, bang and kill,
He got squashed;
No time for his will.

He touched nothing, no alcohol at all.
Unfortunately the driver did;
The driver is alive . . .
                    . . . He died!

Charlotte Ranken (13)
Edgehill College

THE EAGLE

He flies gracefully high in the sky,
above the heads of the awe-struck passers-by.
His wings are spread in a wide arc,
it steals your breath and stops your heart.

He skilfully dives for his food,
what he eats depends on his mood.
He sits on a cactus to eat his snack,
if I were a mouse, I'd watch my back.
For now he's satisfied, but later in the day,
he will eat something else if he has his way.

The day draws on and he is asleep,
he has his eyes closed and is breathing deep.
Everyone has no choice, but to marvel at his skill,
while he dreams of his latest kill.

The sun is visible on the horizon,
he gets up every day at the rising of the sun.
He preens his feathers until they look neat,
then he starts cleaning his clawed feet.

Today will be like yesterday and the day before,
if you want to know what he does each day
read this poem once more.

Melanie Tomlin (13)
Edgehill College

ROLLER-COASTER

Hold on tight!
Wave at Mum,
We're off, we're going,
Ahhh, we're gone!

We'll soon be high,
No need to be shy,
Everyone's gone green,
I wonder why?

The wheels are squeaking,
The carriages are creaking,
We're spinning around and around,
So don't look down!

It's a scream a minute,
I can't believe I did this,
We're touching the sky,
Whose idea was this anyway?

Pretend you're fine,
Try to be brave,
'Here's the sick bag!'
'No, I need an ice-cream!'

Dizzy, still spinning,
'Your stomach still whirling?'
Stumbling and falling,
Laughing and bawling,
It's over you say:
Swearing never again!

'Look there's the waltzers, you coming?'
'Yeah why not!'

Katharine Smaldon (13)
Edgehill College

MY KALEIDOSCOPE

When I was a little boy
It was quite my favourite toy.
All the colours of the rainbow
Merging into patterns that flow.

When the tube is held up high
The pictures glisten in my eye.
Tiny jewel-like pieces of glass,
Merging; flowing till they pass.

When the plastic tube I turn,
Many lessons I do learn.
Things aren't always what they seem,
When through the glass comes a sunbeam.

The patterns, like life, soon go,
They cannot be held I know.
I will enjoy them while I can,
For soon I will be a full grown man.

Then, when I have a small boy,
He too will delight in my toy.
Patterns ever rearranging,
Like the seasons ever changing.

Matthew Braund (12)
Edgehill College

MY HAMSTER SADIE

She's round and fat and
Loved by all
She always comes
When she is called
She's furry and sweet and
Has four tiny feet
But being a hamster
She hates meat
She's ever so cute
When she sleeps in her toy boat
She sleeps all day and
When I get home she wants to play
She runs around on my floor
But never escapes out the door
Her worst enemy
Are my cats
They would chase everything
Including Sadie and my sister's rat
So I keep her safe
Out of harm's way and
With me forever
Is where she will stay.

Kristina Kastelan (12)
Edgehill College

THE POEM

Colours and kaleidoscopes
Elephants in zoos:
I've got to write a poem
But I'm totally confused!
Bubbles in the bath
Flowers in the wood:
I have to hand it in tomorrow,
I'd do it if I could!
Winter and wind
Summer and sun
Sandcastles, leaves and swallows:
It's all a lot of fun!
The pressure's building up,
I'm getting really stuck.
Tonight I just don't feel inspired,
Perhaps it's 'cos I'm tired!

Erin Clarke (12)
Edgehill College

THE HORSE

Wild but peaceful
Cantering into the moonlight
Glazed against the sand
Beating in three time
Pacing every step
The waves crash at his feet.

He quickens his pace
His hair shining brightly
His mane flowing in the wind
His tail beating against the rocks
Visible hoof prints each time he treads.

Slowing down
He makes his retreat
Heading straight for me
Swerving at the last minute
Wild and dangerous.

He runs off leaving only his hoof prints behind.

Rebecca Mudd (12)
Edgehill College

RUGBY

The ball is like an egg:
If you drop it you will lose it,
the other team seizes it,
they will get position,
with the egg
to pass it,
that will score the try,
that will win the game,
to lead them on to glory.

In the scrum we shove and push to get the ball,
to lead us on to glory:
we win the ball,
and then we pass it down the line,
as it goes
the other team race in to run us down,
to get position,
to score the try
that will win the game
to lead them on to glory.

Alexander Foot (12)
Edgehill College

MY PASTIME

I have a little pony
sweet natured as can be.
Black, with two white socks
and her name is 'Tammy'.

Clip, clop, clip, clop
we both go a-trotting.
Up hill and down hill
both our heads a-bobbing.

On our ride we both enjoy
each other's company.
For Tammy is my best friend
with all the love she brings.

Sarah Heard (12)
Edgehill College

DOGGY HAVEN

I know a lakeland terrier
whose name is Algy Pickles.
He makes a funny noise
when given lots of tickles.

His friends Roly Poly, Jo
Bertie, Tobit and Co.
All happen to live in Devon,
you see, Clovelly is doggies' heaven.

They all dawdle off to town
and slowly wander down.
Collecting yummy tit-bits
those silly little nit-wits.

For they didn't really know
that they weren't supposed to go.
Without asking permission
on their canine secret mission.

Naomi Langdon (12)
Edgehill College

AS TIME GOES BY

Do you remember when we were young,
Going to the beach having fun in the sun?
The ice-cream the lollies, going round to
Polly's - wasn't life so much fun?

Do you remember when we were in our teens,
Late nights, the drink and having weird dreams?
Being woken by the alarm clock,
Picked up the wrong sock,
Being late for school,
Making you look like a fool.

And then comes the working stage,
For 40 years you're going to get a wage.
The early mornings, the sleepless nights,
Sometimes life feels just like a fight,
You never win, you always lose.

And now you reach the old age part,
This includes false teeth and sometimes a weak heart.
For the last 60 years you've been working with Sue,
And now for one time in your life,
You have nothing to do.

Charlotte Branch (12)
Edgehill College

A LITTLE FRIEND

I was walking through the woods one day,
And I saw as I went on my way,
A little bird in a bush,
He looked just like a little thrush.

He flew up into a big tree,
And as he perched, he said to me:
'Stay friend and hear me sing,
For my voice out sings anything.'

I replied to him 'What is the worry,
And before you fly in a great flurry,
Tell me why I must hear you sing,
If your voice is greater than anything?'

'Alas, if no one hears me sing,
I may disappear in a ping.
For men could come and capture me,
As I am sitting in my chestnut tree.

And if they captured me,
Whilst sitting in my chestnut tree,
I would have to sing and sing,
If my voice out sings anything.

To people who do not care,
About what it's like out there,
I would be treated as a child's toy,
And that would not fill my heart with joy.'

Sian Lewis (12)
Edgehill College

THE PYRAMID'S SECRET

The sun sets on the Nile's western bank.
Shadows cast themselves across the sandy desert.
The Great Pyramid's silhouette is enchanting,
Against the setting sun.

The red sky's glow is warm and dream-like,
Wafts of Ancient Egypt float past, like puffs of a
Gentle, soothing breeze from an ancient feathered fan
Made from white ostrich down.

The pharaoh sits in a chair of gold,
In his precious throne room. Before him lies a hoard
Of collected gifts. His sacred cat is sitting
Regally at his right.

The pharaoh summons slaves with a small gesture.
They have been ordered to fan him - but wait:-
The picture is fading, fading. As the sun sets,
The picture fades with it.

The wondrous world of Ancient Egypt
Lies on the Nile's western bank. The pharaoh lies
In his pyramid tomb, his world gone, but not lost,
How? I do not know -
For that, my friend, is the pyramid's best kept secret.

Corinne Boyle (12)
Edgehill College

WINTER BECKONS

Light is decreasing quickly,
Dew is rising,
Warmth is fading
and the frosty cold biting.

Soon the mornings will come later,
And evenings sooner.
The frost will set,
Countryside freezes.

Snow will come soon,
Covering everything like a white sheet.
Till spring comes,
Bringing new life and growth.

Hannah Langdon (14)
Edgehill College

AUTUMN

Autumn time is here again,
following the long summer sun.
The nights are pulling in now
leaves brown, orange and yellow.

Roasting chestnuts on the fire,
apple and blackberry pie in the oven.
Bonfires being lit,
the blazing flames on fire.

Crispy, crunchy leaves underfoot,
scarves, coats and gloves.
Deepening skies bring howling, whistling winds
fallen conkers on the ground.

Chimneys full of smoke from the fire
dead flowers and rotten apples.
Falling leaves make empty trees
autumn time is here again!

Della Oliver (12)
Edgehill College

A New Girl At School

When the new girl arrives everyone looks
at her neatly brushed hair and her new bag of books.
First was assembly singing loudly to God
and afterwards into her classroom she trod.
Everyone started to fill out their timetables,
then their clothes were checked for named labels.
From aprons to overalls, from tights to blouses,
then from books to bags, to badges for houses.
After she'd started to learn some kids' names,
they picked up their hockey sticks: it was time for games.
Then trooping round afterwards looking for rooms,
perusing their watches dinner time looms;
When the time comes there's lots of noise,
from the dinner time queue of girls and boys.
After dinner she walks round the grounds looking,
and then gets her apron, the next lesson is cooking.
After doing lots of work she has a sore neck,
then looking at her timetable realises next lesson is tech!
While walking down to tech on the gravel paths,
everyone between themselves talks, chatters and laughs.
At the end of the day she looks up to the sky,
glad it's over but happy; everyone turns and says 'Bye'.

Sophia Walter (12)
Edgehill College

COLOURS OF THE REEF

Gliding through the shallow lagoons,
The sun's rays shine through
Enlightening the seabed
And turning the water a glistening blue.
Flashes of colour, dashing for cover,
Weaving through the reef.
I merge in with the life around me,
More amazing than belief.
Colourful streaks fly around
And jump and swim and burst
Like thousands of rainbows and butterflies.
With the other fish I swiftly meander
Adding to the vibrant scene.

Suzanne Robinson (14)
Edgehill College

MY LOVE

No one will ever realise,
No one will ever know,
That the love I feel for you,
Will never ever go.

You're in my thoughts,
You're in my heart,
And will remain forever,
Until death do us part.

If only you got to know me,
If only you gave me a chance,
Just maybe I'd mean something to you
And you'd give me a second glance.

Some day you'll love me,
Some day you'll care,
I'll wait for that day,
Our lives we can share.

Jo-anne Sime (14)
Edgehill College

FOOTBALL

Football is fun
When played in the sun.
But football is slimy
When dirty and grimy.
I like to stay clean.

Football's a bore
Unless you can score.
Then it's a laugh
Before the bath.
I like to be clean.

Football's a dream
It's played with a team
We all pull together
Regardless of weather.
I like to be dry.

Shoot, punt or pass
It's all played on grass.
Fat, short or tall
It's eyes on the ball.
The thing is to try.

Oliver Mellor (11)
Edgehill College

THE MURDER OF A ROSE

The hot, hot days of summer are fading,
Clouds fill the sky with gloom,
Soon Jack Frost will visit.
The garden is covered by a sheeting,
To protect the soil, and few remaining plants.

One rose, red as blood,
Is blown out from beneath the sheet.
A breath of ice-cold wind blows;
He has arrived with winter on his back
And hovers by each bare tree,
Turned to stone, left with coats of ice and frost.

The single rose, uncovered, is tickled by his fingers,
He smiles a wicked smile and dashes up into the sky.
The rose, once red as blood,
Lies dead on a resting bed of mud.
Frozen petals curled up in sadness,
The rose is left to Rest In Peace.

Claire Stevens (14)
Edgehill College

AUTUMN

As winter approaches
The days are less warm;
The nights draw in quickly
And curtains are drawn.

The trees become bare,
The leaves turn to gold;
The sky swirling blue
- a sight to behold.

Colours of russet, amber and bronze
Cover the earth like a rug.
Leaves crunch and crackle, lawns crisp with frost,
A glut of ripe fruit in the trug.

Birds will migrate to lands far away,
Fireworks light up the sky.
Hedgehogs sleep soundly right up to the spring,
God's gift of a season gone by.

Sophie Barker (14)
Edgehill College

JUST LISTEN

People say it's good to be different.
They say I'm great, just how I am,
But that's because they can't say
Anything else to this broken, silent body.

They seem to exclude me from Normal People.
They try to pretend I'm not even there,
Just because my face, my arms, my legs
Don't work as other people's do.

I'm like a silent statue
Listening to every word.
They think I can't hear them
Talking of what they've heard.

If I could talk like Normal People
The first thing I would say is,
'There's a soul inside this body -
Please don't let it rot away.'

Joanna Foot (15)
Edgehill College

YOU ARE

You are all I think about all day
You are my first thought in the morning
You are my last thought at night
You are my sweet dream as I sleep
You are my sun, moon and stars
You are the person for whom I would do anything
You are what keeps me going
You are perfect in every way
You are honest, kind and beautiful
You are the funniest, most outrageous person I know
You have the ability to make me smile
You are caring, sensitive and loving
You are always calm and happy
You are colourful and brighten my day
You are like sunshine after a storm
You are like a fire on a cold day
You are always aware of how I feel
You are generous and make me feel special
You are the person to whom my heart belongs
You are able to possess it forever, and longer
You are the one I will love eternally
You are all I want and need
You are all this, simply because,
You are you.

Anna Forbes (14)
Edgehill College

INFANT SORROW

I plod up the stairs with heavy feet.
My head is bowed low.
I climb headfirst into bed, my crumpled sheet,
I cry never-ending tears of sorrow.
There is no longer hope without my mum,
I don't know how I'll cope.
I lie awake, waiting,
For Mum to come and tuck me into bed.
But I know in my heart
She is never coming back.
We buried her, put apple blossoms
Over her head.
Without her, the world seems black.

No one changes my sheets,
Dad is preoccupied,
He has been for weeks.
We sit on the sofa, together we cry.
The weeks seem endless,
The months drag by.
There's an empty place in my heart
Where Mum used to be,
As if I've been pierced by a flying dart.
For as long as I live,
I will remember her.
She was here
Because she had something to give.

Ayesha Loveridge (16)
Edgehill College

SOMEONE TO BURN

What shall you do? There's nothing to do,
About illness, and starving and dying.
What shall you do? There's nothing to do.
Nothing but swearing and lying.
Find someone to hurt.
Let them go up in smoke.
Burn all your troubles away.

Sometimes it's monsters, but what will you choose?
Sometimes it's mad men - lock them away.
It's races and sexes and even it's Jews,
Would you truly be happy if they all went away?
Find someone to hurt.
Let them go up in smoke.
Burn all your troubles away.

If you had the choice to kill or to save,
Would you help the weak and the sick?
Or would you turn away from the begging of slaves,
Running for shelter from the lick of a whip?
Find someone to hurt.
Let them go up in smoke.
Burn all your troubles away.

Confront all the evils this world has to throw,
Giving as good as you can get.
Take all your worries and put on a show,
About avoiding all obstacles and winning the bet.
Find someone to love.
Help them rise up with joy.
Let them fly to the stars and away.

Becky Hartley (16)
Edgehill College

KALEIDOSCOPE

A myriad of changing colours,
A myriad of patterns of light and of shapes.
Patterns intricate in their infinity.

The changing of the seasons,
Summer, spring, winter and autumn.
Forever changing in an endless cycle.

The ever-changing weather,
There is the wind, the rain, the hail and the snow.
What it will be? You will never know.

Life is a kaleidoscope!
How it will turn out,
You can never know.

A billion patterns,
Each one different,
There are patterns of light, of shapes, even patterns of patterns.

Life is full of the little things,
It is the little things that matter.
Each one is unique, just like the bits in a kaleidoscope.

What we do one day will affect another;
You can find a beautiful pattern,
Or, of course, you can miss it.

But there is one rule,
And it governs all of our lives;
The kaleidoscope's and ours -
There is no turning back!

Oliver Harris (12)
Edgehill College

On The Beach

I lie on my towel and look up at the sky,
Watching all the kites that fly.

The sound of the sea roaring in my ear,
Children's voices very near.

I dig my toes into the sand,
And picture the lifeguard holding my hand.

The sun is burning on my face,
Seaside donkeys at a slow pace.

Soggy, sandy sandwiches, leaky flasks,
Tarts in bikinis bouncing past.

Cricket, tennis and volleyball,
On the beach they play them all.

Holly Castle (13)
Edgehill College

My View On A Certain Sport

There is a sport I will not name
but to me I feel
it is quite lame.

People support it most of all sports
and all it requires is a T-shirt and shorts.

The players get paid
huge amounts of
cash all because
of their 90-minute dash.

But still all boys
think it's cool
to play the game we call
   Football.

Paul Pratt (14)
Edgehill College

MEMORIES
(This poem may not make much sense to the reader, but for one person
it holds a great importance and it is for that person it is written)

The window we sat at once,
is broken and fallen to dust.
The vines tangle around the frame,
my memories are all in vain.

My lost memories of the sun;
of him and me; foolishness and fun.
We used to sit for hours on end,
and watch the mighty ball descend.

We saw it rise we saw it fall,
his love I hardly felt at all.
My life reflected in its power;
now under the sun I do cower.

Its rays we watched from dawn till dusk,
till they were shrouded, lost in dust.
The beautiful window I once loved,
is hidden and lost in his hatred and lust.

Phillip Clayton (14)
Edgehill College

QUAKE

From level to level,
Gun to gun,
I kill all the bad guys.

It's cool this gun,
A missile launcher,
They don't have a chance.

Yahoo! Completed,
I'm on level nine,
I've never been here before.

I'm fresh out of ammo,
I'm not going too well,
And where is that rune key I need?

I'm going to die.
I don't have a chance.
But wait, it's that gold key at last.

Oh no! It's the boss.
Oh man, he is big.
Eat lead you stupid monster!

'Ryan, your hour is up.'
'But Mum.'
Oh, it's not fair.

Ryan Kewley (12)
Edgehill College

PEOPLE

People are happy
People are sad

People are dull
People are bad

So why not be one of us
And be happy but not too sad

People are humorous
Responsible and cheerful

And always say hello
When they are tearful

So always have a happy face
And then the world will be a happy place

Catherine Verney (14)
Edgehill College

FIRE

Fire, a twisting jumping puzzle of heat.
Fire is like an angry source forcing into empty
spaces smothering everything.
Fire is a sudden unknown movement with its
thick, black, breathtaking smoke filling the air.
It's an unstoppable power taking everything in
its path.
Calm and swift is a small little flame but as it feeds
on oxygen it can become a life-taking force.

Ben Mansell (13)
Exeter School

NO-MAN'S-LAND

A hundred yards of hell:
Blasted and battered and bruised by
Numberless screaming shells;
Littered with long strings of sharp,
Biting, curled, springing wire.
The once green meadows
Swept daily dirtier by the pointless
Streams of machine-gun bullets.
War, like a playful giant, has
Torn apart the peace of countless years.
This garden of ours bordered by the
Hellish tombs-to-be of Hades:
Trenches, filled to the stinking brim
With hapless soldiers, breathing but dead.
This is no man's land.

Tom Littler (14)
Exeter School

HALF-ASLEEP

My eyelids are heavy,
But not closed,
Words drift in,
And out again,
My dazzled mind,
Reflects back on time,
And back it goes,
To childhood days.

My vision is dazzled,
In this present world,
But memories float clearly,
Throughout my head,
As stories, pictures, sounds return,
Of joyful days,
And gloomy days,
A sudden movement,
Makes me jump,
And brings me back to reality,
With a bump.

Thomas Bignell (12)
Exeter School

FIRE

Fire - man's oldest foe.
Swirling patterns.
Hot as the sun.
An enigma of orange limbs.
Melting and destroying anything in its path.
Bright and powerful.
Warm in the night.
Flickers in the wind.
Raging, but then still.
Glowing bricks of heat.

Water its only nemesis,
Steam its child.
Fire is pleasure but also torture.
Fire is beautiful but also dangerous.

Will Maltby (14)
Exeter School

THE BATTLE

Theseus entered the cave,
Gore of dead bodies o'erwhelmed him,
Pools of blood flooded the cave,
Broken weapons scattered round him.

From behind a massive rock,
Out jumped the awful Minotaur,
Through the dismal light and horrible gore,
Appeared the roaring Minotaur.

Through the dark night the battle raged until,
Light-footed and swiftly turning,
Theseus our hero with mighty sword,
Charged and slashed, killing the Minotaur.

Lawrence Millett (11)
Exeter School

NO-MAN'S-LAND

A new world has taken shape between us and the enemy,
One of death and fear,
A land shaped by man and his creation - war, and crafted with mud.
Rivers flow through this unpleasant land,
Rivers of blood and water - a stagnant cocktail,
Men lie half-buried, struck down by men just like them,
The charred remains of trees are all that is left of the land before,
They too, like animals that made their homes here, are casualties of
man.
All the men who lie here dead and disfigured have gone to a better
place,
Heaven or Hell.

Tom Hoar (14)
Exeter School

HOME THOUGHTS FROM THE FRONT: WISH YOU WERE HERE!

This is what it's like
To look Death in the eyes.
To see grown men cower like urchins
In the hell that is reality.

This is what it's like
To see a corpse in pieces.
Devoid of identity;
A useless hunk of meat.

This is what it's like
To be so cold
Your joints are frozen solid
And you wish you were dead.

This is what it's like
To be herded like a dumb sheep
Through a world of mud and blood
And a world of misery and darkness.

This is what it's like
To be so totally alone
Alienated from sanity
Separated from civilization.

This is what it's like
This is War.

Nick Bowen (14)
Exeter School

THE REALITY OF WAR

Hell on earth, the soldiers' trench
A hundred yards away from death
A hundred young men, shocked and drenched
At the mercy of their General's wrath

Thick black mud, an oily slime
That slips between the fighters' feet
The crack of rifles, machine-gun fire
Makes the cacophony complete

The barbed wire marks the walls of their prison
In front lies an almost-certain end
Behind, the Colonels are safely hidden
From horrors they cannot comprehend

The folk back home have no understanding -
Think war is just a glorified game
'Fight for a cause that you believe in!'
Have they never heard of pain?

Benjamin King (14)
Exeter School

VICTORY

The trigger is pulled
He falls
Anger and evil lie dark upon the battlefield
No blade of grass
Nor man stirs
A long saddened silence encloses the musty smell of death
Blood trickles from the open wound
It drops upon the darkened grass
A siren wails in the distance
Some planes fly low
The bombs land
And bomblets scatter over men
Explosions fire right and left
Earth, grass, blows on the breeze
So many dead
So few alive
Hope of victory in the mind
The alive triumph
No more fighting
But yet no peace
Men, women, children
Dead.

Thomas Renninson (11)
Exeter School

DEADLY ADVENTURE

The den towers above,
I see bones,
I see blood,
I see . . .
The Minotaur,
He looms above,
So big, so strong,
The stench so bad,
Like dirt and decomposed bodies,
The snorting of the Minotaur,
Deafens and echoes,
He grabs for me,
He feels as hard as stone,
I taste sharp sour blood,
Overwhelming me,
Bloodshot eyes stare at me,
Shaking ground,
As he stampedes at me,
I jump,
Crack,
His horns stuck in the wall
Slice, swirl,
Down the Minotaur goes,
Lying lifelessly,
Dead.

Matthew Pennington (11)
Exeter School

THE FIGHT

I step into the
Fetid air of the
Minotaur's den.

I see green gangrene,
Decaying flesh from
Victims past.

A roar and it's
Upon me. Breathing
Hate from flaming nostrils.

Swords swinging,
Thrusting, slashing,
I meet the threat.

Hot red blood,
Pouring from its
Body. A final breath,
It's dead. I've won.

Tim Lee (12)
Exeter School

THE FIGHT

The blue eyes of mine,
The bloodshed of his,
The clash of sword and bone,
The gore is scattered around,
And the guts and gore,
As the battle continued.

The smell of his vile breath,
And his deafening roar,
His furry hand around my neck,
I am thrown back against the wall,
It started to go black, but I held
Myself together,
As the battle continued.

This bull towering over me,
Blood pouring out of his eye,
A fist fell into my face,
Overpowering me backwards,
Lunging with my sword,
Going through the beast,
And he crawled away, wounded.

Matthew Powell (11)
Exeter School

How I Killed The Minotaur

M y heart beats like a drum,
I feel weak and scared,
N othing is moving or making a sound as I walk
    towards my doom.
O ther bodies lay in my way,
T heir flesh hanging off their bones.
A ll I can see is the sleeping Minotaur,
U gly, disgustingly huge.
R unning towards him I raised my sword . . .

and

T he Minotaur awoke and with a grunt and a
    snort it lunged towards me.
H is fur felt tough and wiry on my smooth skin as
    I closed my arms around his neck.
E ffort upon effort we fought to the death.
S our blood cringed in my mouth, the drool
    dropped from his jaw.
E merald and topaz colours flashed before me as he
    spun me around the cave.
U p came my sword, right through his head, his
    bloodshot eyes closed as he roared and died.
S taggering across the cave I rested against a rock,
    leaving my wounds to heal.

Adam Pill (11)
Exeter School

THE FIGHT WITH THE MINOTAUR

As I walked into the
Minotaur's den,
I could smell a musty smell,
Like rotting flesh.
I looked on the floor and it
Was littered with corpses.
The sights shocked me of
Those who had been slain.
There were bats hanging
Above my head,
Rats were scuttling around
My feet.
Then I heard an eerie sound,
The sound came again more
Like a roar.
I turned quickly and there
Behind me, stood the Minotaur.
We started to fight,
He was strong and I was
Weak.
He soon had me in his grasp,
I let out a shriek of fear
Then with sudden movement
I pulled out my sword.
I ploughed it right through
His heart.

I jumped back.
He fell with an agonising cry.
I looked down at him,
His eyes were pained and then,
They closed.
There was rich red blood
Oozing about my feet.

Stuart Holman (11)
Exeter School

THE BATTLE

Broken weapons
Broken bones,
The Minotaur roars
And the Minotaur groans.

The Minotaur snorts
As he advances,
Theseus looks
Around in glances.

But there is no way out
For he is cornered,
Theseus shouts
And charges forward.

Giant horns and swords are clashing
Theseus hacks at the Minotaur's head,
Echoing around the big dark den
The Minotaur falls for he is dead.

Tim Black (11)
Exeter School

BATTLE WITH THE MINOTAUR

Turning the corner,
I peered into the cave,
I could tell that I was close to him,
For the bones of the brave,
Were scattered on the floor,
In the Athenians' early grave.

He turned round suddenly,
His face masked in gore,
Bloodshot eyes,
Stinking breath,
Powerful muscular arms,
And smelling of death.

I struck the first blow,
Trying to hit hard,
It glanced off his horn,
Hit the wall and jarred,
Then he lunged,
Caught my arm,
Blood trickled free,
I started to shiver,
As he charged at me.

I leapt to the left,
He careered on past,
One chance,
Act fast,
Strike,
Dead at last.

Robert Horton (11)
Exeter School

THE FIGHT

Bones dressed with gore lay everywhere,
The Minotaur's eyes were bloodshot,
Blood seeped from the Minotaur's mouth,
Theseus, he was so hot.

Grinning skulls stared forward,
Upon the floor were sharp, spiky stones,
Theseus stumbled and rolled,
The Minotaur roared and there were moans and groans.

Theseus and the Minotaur charged,
The Minotaur was sticky with sweat and blood,
His fur was warm, wiry and soft,
The bones on the floor were like a flood.

Theseus swung his mighty sword,
The Minotaur stepped back and spoke his piece,
'Don't kill me, I won't eat anyone again.'
Whoosh went the sword, that made the fighting cease.

Theseus was the hero of the day,
They wound their way back through the maze,
Leaving his mighty sword behind,
Theseus, he got all the praise.

Lee Palmer (11)
Exeter School

THE BATTLE

The musty smell reached his nose,
He could tell that he was near.
Terror struck him coldly,
He gripped his sword tightly.
Slowly he walked into the cave,
The Minotaur before him.

Sticky sweat rolled down his face,
The dead and the dying lay astrew.
Turning he saw it,
Bigger than he expected.
Horns, teeth and hooves.

He swung his sword in terror,
But his foe was faster.
The sharp taste of blood was in his mouth.
The Minotaur lowered his head to charge,
Theseus struck home and the Minotaur was dead.

Matthew Tyrer (11)
Exeter School

HEAT

Ice
The door slams shut
All safely inside, away from the harsh wind

Coats are dismissed
Now unwanted, sodden hats and gloves are thrown on the floor
But layers of clothing are still kept on
Nobody is warm yet

Heading into the glowing kitchen
They watch as the rain cascades to the ground
But in their 'little bubble' they are safe

Now layers of clothing are pulled off
'Pins and needles' in the hands show progress
A steaming mug of hot chocolate burns the tips of their tongues

One hour later, everyone is warm
Even hot
Ice cubes are put in drinks
Heat.

Robert Grieg-Gran (13)
Exeter School

FIRE

Fire is like a trapped creature struggling to escape,
The red light melts your eyes as it feeds on wood
and coal.
The tremendous heat swallows the coal as the fire
increases.
Singing, melting and burning as the tongues of fire
deal with whatever gets in its path,
Alarm bells ring out as the innocent victims cry out
for their lives.
The fire has finished its meal,
There is no more to burn.
The red-hot ashes remain,
With a touch of water the ashes reply with a large
hiss.

Damien Mansell (13)
Exeter School

LEAVING THE FRONT

A grey snake slithers through the trenches
It fumbles and gropes in the morning quiet
A flare goes up, the tin scales glisten
Then it plunges back into the sickening void

A train of men, merely marching corpses
Trudge on with the curdled mud sucking their heels
And the numbing emptiness continues
Within every returning soul.

Fabien Flight (14)
Exeter School

GUY FAWKES NIGHT

I watched the rocket go up.
It has the speed of a jet,
The elegance of a silk cat.

It climbed the everlasting ladder,
Until it reached its destiny.
It exploded with the might of a tiger,
And the beauty of a panda.

Its little offspring shone brightly in the dark night sky,
They floated down slowly as if each and every one of them
were clinging on to an invisible parachute.

Eventually it reaches the ground,
And with a disturbing groan it lets out its last bit of light energy.

Then the next rocket is given its spark of life,
And the cycle starts again.

Chris Horne (13)
Exeter School

ENERGETIC DOG

Long muscular legs glide through the slippery wet grass.
He hears a rustle in the brambles.
His ears point up and his hair stands on edge.
He stops and waits in silence.
He sprints so fast, as fast as he can go,
So fast you can hardly see him.
Ten minutes later he comes back empty-handed and puffed out.

Cara Horrell (14)
Great Torrington School

THE ELEGANT HORSE

Cantering round with her head held
high,
The power in her legs,
Oh, I wish she could fly.

Her long silky mane,
Shining in the light,
Her pure black coat,
What a wonderful sight.

She comes towards me with a look in
her eye,
Then runs away,
without saying goodbye.

I will never see a thing so fine,
I wish the elegant horse was mine.

Jessica May (13)
Great Torrington School

THE CAT AND JEALOUSY

Jealousy is a trait that is fearful.
The cat is a jealous being.
She wanders through the dark of night
Waiting for her prey.

Her eyes look from left to right,
From right to left again.
Another cat approaches her.
She never comes again.

Sarah Ford (13)
Great Torrington School

THE SNAKE

The sly snake slithers through the grass
Always knowing what he will pass.
Sneaking waiting to catch his prey,
Nearly waiting all the day.

He spots a meal way up high
And then the bird comes swooping by.
With one lash of its fangs it
Brings the bird down with many bangs.

He won his meal, now he can rest
Knowing now he must be the best.
He goes and takes one big bite
Not knowing that he's in for a fight.

Paul Elkins (13)
Great Torrington School

THE SNAKE

The snake is sleek
But strong
It never attacks wrong
His fangs are sharp
His scales are smooth
They slither along the floor
Just to find their prey
Silent attacker, motionless
Seemingly asleep
The cocked spring explodes
The prey is caught.

Riki Johnson (13)
Great Torrington School

THE ALLIGATOR

The alligator is hungry,
He is looking for some food,
He has great power in his jaws.
As he goes into the water,
He takes a bush out with one swipe of
his giant tail.
He slides into the water to find some fish.
As he glides through the water,
He sees fish jumping to catch flies.
He picks up speed and makes after them,
With power coming from his tail
He races under the water.
He catches a mouthful of fish,
And with one mighty gulp
He swallows the lot.
Then, when he is satisfied,
He clambers back onto the bank
For his midday nap.

Darren Redford (13)
Great Torrington School

THE UFO

My telescope's out, oh what a sight,
What could that be?
That flash of eye-blinding light,
Look at that, that can't be right.
It's probably because it's a dark, dark night,
Or perhaps it was a shooting star
That gave me a fright,
Or, was it a UFO in flight . . . ?

Robert Lee (12)
Great Torrington School

DOLPHIN SO SHY

Dolphin swimming through the water
So peaceful, full of grace
Its long smooth nose
Its body so long
But he doesn't always
Come about to shout
He is so shy
But no one can tell
He is so graceful
In the water
If you see him
You can go home
Then tell your friends
Of this sleek, shy
But graceful animal.

Sarah Heywood (13)
Great Torrington School

THE SHY ZEBRA

Her sad eyes look at the floor,
Her stripy skin makes you notice her more,
She walks along on her own,
She's sometimes with a herd,
But mostly on her own,
She looks so distant,
She looks so calm.
She has many friends,
Her little face, her little eyes
She looks as though she wants to cry.

Francine Downton (14)
Great Torrington School

AGGRESSIVE CROCODILE

Scaly skin and sharp teeth,
In the water he slides,
Underneath the water,
Right under the shade.

He watches his prey,
Still and very quiet,
Then suddenly he pounces,
Snap, snap, snap!
He misses.
The prey gets away.
He slips back under the water,
Immobile log, deceptive and discreet,
He still touches his prey,
He may not eat for hours or even for days.

Gemma Robinson (13)
Great Torrington School

THE FIERCE LION

The fierce lion stalks his prey,
Creeping through the tall brown grass.
He waits a while watching the antelope with eager eyes.
The antelope still, listening for a movement.
The lion creeps further forward waiting for the
right moment to strike.
Bang! The lion pulls his victim down.
The lion engages his claws in the victim.
Blood running down the side of this innocent victim.
The lion starts to eat his way through the prey,
His mouth stained with scarlet blood.

Lewis Parker (13)
Great Torrington School

SILENT EYES

Silent eyes, devoid of mercy,
Watching intently, calmly and perfect,
Browny-black diamonds, creeping up its back,
Sharp pointed tail, spade-shaped head.
Silent eyes, devoid of mercy,
Spots its doomed prey.
Strong, bunched muscles, waiting to spring,
Forked tongue, tasting in motion, tastes the fear of death.
Prey is in reach, the trap is sprung!
Muscles let loose, the slender body fires forward,
Deadly fangs, shot forward by organic pistons.
They deliver their payload with pinpoint accuracy,
Silent eyes, ablaze with the fire of glory.

Ross Mitchell (14)
Great Torrington School

SNAKE

A snake creeps up through the grass.
Can be as sneaky as we are.
He sees his prey, he goes for it
sneaking up fast and quick.
The snake slithers around so silent and
calm.
He sees an egg he thinks tasty so he
goes for it so silent in the wind.
He sneaks up round the tree
crunch, crunch - that's it.

James Pyke (13)
Great Torrington School

TRAP-DOOR SPIDER

The eight black and brown hairy legs make the trap.
The seven hexagonal eyes stare and wait.
The feeling of *doom* is in the air.
The sweet smell of revenge is wafting around.
Then the innocent four-winged creature passes near.
Anxious for food, the spider gets apprehensive in his every move.
Boom! The trap-door shuts and he catches his prey.
There is no chance of escape for the poor creature.
The spider goes in for the kill . . .
The poor innocent creature is gone.
The spider has his prey at last.
The devious, cunning plan has worked.
He has no need for food,
Until the next time . . .

Jamie Thompson (13)
Great Torrington School

THE CAT

Curled up, dormant by the fire,
The flame flickering gently in his big green eyes.
He stretches out and yawns a yawn
and smiles with his eyes.
He spies the anger in my pose,
hands on hips, my head shaking.
He jumps up quick and purrs round my legs so lovingly.
My anger melts, he is so innocent in his eyes.
Yet he knows it.
How he manipulates my love to his own ends.
The cat.

Susie Williams (13)
Great Torrington School

THE GRACEFUL CAT

The cat, so wonderfully adapted to catch prey,
The way it crouches ready to pounce,
Triumphantly, tail in the air,
Prize in the mouth.
It is graceful in its every way.
The way it walks over the dewy grass,
Then shakes the droplets off its paws.
Its ears so delicate and graceful,
In its every twitch and turn.
The way it sits,
Ears pricked,
Piercing eyes shut.
Every strand of soft fur in its place,
There is no animal more graceful
than the cat.

Claire Ashton (14)
Great Torrington School

PROTECTION

Pacing up and down.
Prowling his territory.
Defending his area
From other animals.
Protecting his owner from dangers
Alert and wary of who and what
passes by.
Getting ready to pounce upon
unwelcome guests.

Helen Laney (13)
Great Torrington School

LIONESS

The eyes
are big and red
Eyes glowing
at the victim
Her big powerful
legs tense so
She can spring
on her victim.

She is golden
she has so much camouflage
She looks like
long golden grass.

She is the
strongest of the lions
If you can get to
her.

She is the
queen of evil
And the jungle
ruler.

So watch your back
she is so sly
She could get you quicker
than you think!

Nicky Hymas (13)
Great Torrington School

FEARLESS SHARK

The famous Great White
Scared of nothing and feared by everything.
Its gaping jaws swallowing its prey,
Its dark blue eyes staring into nothing but water,
Swimming into the shallowest waters
and lurking in dark gloomy seas.
Many things become its victim
including the great killer whale.
They hunt together like fearless wolves
devouring innocent rabbits,
Attacking ships and jolly boats.
There are not many survivors.
The fearless shark so strong and limitless
patrols the sea like a guard.

James Mathews (13)
Great Torrington School

THE LONELY

The little dormouse scared and unseen
Although it's somewhere.
It's like a little child with no friends.
Only comes out when food is at hand.
It does not speak or make contact with life.
Wary of who and what goes by.
So scared it cannot sleep at night.
In the day it is very lonely.
It sits in its little house like a child
that's learnt not to trust.

Cleo Bott (13)
Great Torrington School

THE BIG ISSUE!

I'm homeless.
It's cold and raining.
Someone walks past me,
I say 'Do you want to buy the Big Issue?'
But they just ignore me.
Then it starts to thunder.
I'm cold.
Lots of people walk past.
I hope that someone will buy
The Big Issue off me.
But they don't.
I'm cold
and I want to go home.

Karla Bissett (12)
Great Torrington School

IN MY CHAIR

Here I sit in my chair,
People walk by
And all of them stare.
I ask myself and wonder why,
I am so different
And start to cry.
Day after day
I will be there,
Because I am homeless
And have no one to care.

Timothy Brush (12)
Great Torrington School

THE COUNTRYSIDE

Way down deep,
Where the bales are stacked steep,
The green green grass
Every day I go past.

In the field where the animals lay,
With straw to feed and hay for their bay,
With hedges to keep them in,
For their own safety.

I live in the countryside,
It's a bit on the bumpy side,
With all the farms,
It's quiet and calm.

Charlene Potts (12)
Great Torrington School

GHOST

Ghost ghost in the machine
Out you came and I did scream.
I said hello but you went *boo*
When I ran all the way to the zoo.

When I came back I thought you would attack,
But when I came back you jumped on my back.
I wrestled you to the washing machine,
And pushed you in to make you clean.

Jack Elliott (12)
Great Torrington School

DOLPHIN

Dolphin friend I hear you call through the ocean deep.
I look down under and see you
Rushing fast through your friends' feet.

Dolphin friends are kind
Kinder than some people in my mind
Many times I see dolphins in my sleep
Swimming in the ocean deep.

Dolphins in the ocean under my feet
I hear the rushing water down in the deep
Many things rushing through my feet
Then dolphins scoop you up from underneath.

I hear the fastness of the dolphin
When it swims across the ocean deep
And I am crying in my sleep.

Zoey Cook (13)
Great Torrington School

SANTA

The 25th of December has again come around,
Santa creeps in without making a sound,
His reindeers are tethered to the gatepost outside,
I hope all children sleep soundly inside.

Little red stockings hung upon a shelf,
Waiting to be filled by Santa himself,
Nuts and sweets are put inside,
Away Santa goes for another ride.

The next house comes into sight,
Curtains drawn, windows black in the night,
Several more children wait with delight,
Hoping that Santa's coming tonight.

Santa's happy now he's finished his round,
Away he goes, he's homeward bound.
He has to wait without a sound,
Until next year comes around.

Jenny Preece (12)
Great Torrington School

HOMELESS

I am all alone, cold and dark
Pull my blanket over my head.
My blanket is my trusty friend
I hide and dream of other places
            far away
Where it is warm, light, soft and cosy
Awoken by the morning traffic
To start another day alone
Millions of people around but nobody
            there for me.
My days are like long tunnels never ending
Wander the streets begging for money
What will be my next meal?
Dusk begins to fall
another night to get through
cold alone and *homeless.*

Lisa Mitchell (13)
Great Torrington School

DENTIST

Sitting in the dentist's chair,
really gives you quite a scare.
He's like a monster from your sleep,
or a creature from the ocean deep.

Coming at you with his drill,
you try hard just to keep still.
Drilling half your tooth away,
on his special chair you lay.

Finally time for you to go home,
wash your mouth out with pinkish foam.
You step out into the rain,
dreading the day when it starts again.

Natalie Oliver (13)
Great Torrington School

THE NIGHT SKY

Dark and dreary, wet and cold,
Stars glittering silver and gold.
The moon glowing nice and white,
Shooting stars very bright.

I saw a planet, it was Mars,
Shining brighter than all the stars.
I looked up high and felt alone,
I turned around and ran straight home.

Claire Harriss (13)
Great Torrington School

Memory Loss

I can't remember my daughter's face,
I don't know my own name.

My memory's fading, why oh why,
Is it because it's time to die?

Would I be better dead and gone?
Sitting here I'm no use to anyone.

There's my wife, what is her name?
Somehow I think she is ashamed.

I used to laugh, I used to play,
All of these memories are fading away.

Anne-Marie Redford (12)
Great Torrington School

Faces

Isn't it amazing how,
All faces are different, wow.
Fat ones, round ones,
Rosy ones and thin ones.
Fat nose, beady eyes,
Some eyes that tell lies,
Some faces are grumpy
Others are lumpy,
Some are always bright,
And others reflect the light.

Holly Clerc-De-Saux (13)
Great Torrington School

US ON EARTH

Grease and grime in the air,
Killing nature everywhere,
Sewage pouring into the sea,
Animals are unhappy.

People chopping down trees,
To be shipped across seas,
Animals left without a home,
And a plain patch all alone.

People want a new road
Next to the home of fish, frogs and toads
Soon the habitat will die,
Killing nature without saying 'Bye.'

Ozone layer's been damaged,
Soon people won't manage.
People and animals become ill,
Soon there'll be nothing left to kill.

Sarah Mills (13)
Great Torrington School

AUTUMN

Golden coloured leaves floating from the trees,
Blowing in the breeze,
The rustle of the leaves along the ground,
They fell from the trees and then they were found,
Purple, red and orange sunset,
The best view anyone can get.

Children in the country picking fruit,
Walking through the lanes with their loot,
Squirrels collect their winter store,
Other animals looking for more,
Always prepared for the winter ahead,
They lay their heads in a cosy bed.

Michelle Ellis (13)
Great Torrington School

THE TRUTH IS OUT THERE!

Flying over the blue and green,
You'd like to know the things I've seen.
You'll never know, you might not care,
But I know just what is out there.
I've travelled far, beyond your mind,
Things I've found, you'll never find.
The plants I've seen, you'll never sow,
The herbs I tried, you'll never know.
The spice I've tried, beyond compare,
You'll never know what is out there.
The mates I've had, those crazy nights,
You'll never see on satellite.
Go out of your head, expand your mind,
You'll never know what you might find.
So when you're old and in your chair,
Always remember the truth is out there.

Grace Hicks (13)
Great Torrington School

DREAM

A car, a boat, a train, a plane
Yes, I'm off travelling again
Only thoughts dreams unravel.

The car is red, sporty and fast
The boat, it has at least three masts
The train, a steam locomotive, of course
The plane, a fast jet from the Air Force.

I travel here, I travel there
Where only the brave may dare
To travel perhaps a dangerous way
Only the ramblings of dreams may say.

On and on, up and down
Faster, faster, going round
Suddenly things are slowing down
Got to get my feet back on the ground.

Suddenly stillness and quiet is all
Awake or asleep?
I hear a call.
'Come on and get up. It's here, it's here.'
The bus, just what I feared!

Ben Jackson (13)
Great Torrington School

THE EVENING IN OUR STREET

The shadows lengthen,
The air turns cold,
The sun sets,
The day's secrets have been told.

The flowers sleep,
The building's quiet,
The sweet smell,
The finished riot.

The lonely factories,
The whispering trees,
The gentle wind,
Rustles their leaves.

The birds sing,
The river rushes,
The wind combs
The grass like brushes.

The children asleep,
The roads bare
The wires hang
Like great lengths
Of hair.

The sheep eating,
The clouds turning dim,
The sheep's song,
Like some sort of hymn.

Bryony Maycock (12)
Great Torrington School

THE FOUR SEASONS

Spring

Bulbs begin to grow,
The flowers begin to show.
The trees come into bud,
And the lambs play in the mud.

Summer

The midday sun scorches down,
All the sunbathers are very brown!
The bees buzz from flower to flower.
They do this routine every hour.

Autumn

The apples are red,
The leaves are dead.
All the animals have gone to bed.

Winter

The frost descends on the grass below,
Jack Frost has been, there'll soon be snow!

John Woollacott (13)
Great Torrington School

MY STAR VIEW

As I look up to the stars,
I sit here in my four seater car,
I see them shine,
And wish they were mine.

I would take them home,
And I would never moan,
But they would be missed,
So they're back on my dream list.

Sarah Beer (12)
Great Torrington School

AT THE BACK OF MY MIND

A s I look up at the sky
T he puffy clouds wander by.

T oday the stars are shining bright
H eaven made this sparkling light
E ven now it's a ravishing sight.

B eneath the sea where she would stand
A young woman so tall, so grand
C ome talk to me she would say
K nock on the palace door if you want to play.

O utside is another world
F ear and hatred make toes curl.

M agic and mystery, a trick for the eyes
Y et we believe it and know it lies.

M emories thrown from here and there
I n my mind they're there to share
N evertheless they're here to stay
D aring to come out and play.

Tarnya Davies (12)
Great Torrington School

CHRISTMAS TIME

People sing carols around a tree,
Opening presents all in glee,
Lights and tinsel fill up the room,
Third World children sit around
In doom.

Crackers bang, fairies hang.
People sit round hand in hand.
Eating turkey, hats on heads.
People are happy as they are
All fed.

People play games, having no shame
As Third World people don't have
These same *aims*.

While our perfect gift would be a
Nintendo.
Theirs would be a warm house
For the winter.

Thomas Blight (13)
Great Torrington School

CARDBOARD BOX CITY

Cardboard Box City is a poor place,
Where you never see a happy face,
Hunger and cold haunt the people there,
No one cares, it seems so unfair,
Where stealing and begging takes place,
Cardboard Box City is such a poor place.

Claire Whitehouse (12)
Great Torrington School

CHRISTMAS EVE

The clock chimes at twelve
I can't get to sleep
My mind is racing.
I can't wait for the morning
All is quiet in the still of the night
Except my sister who I can hear snoring.
If only I were asleep
Then it would be morning.
My eyes are getting heavy
I think I'm getting sleepy.
The next thing I hear is
My sister shouting 'It's morning.'
Hurray, it's Christmas Day.

Samantha Paine (12)
Great Torrington School

AUTUMN

Autumn is a time of crispy golden leaves,
Falling from the trees,
When animals snuggle up and bury up in a bundle of bracken,
The cold wind blows, the clouds turn grey,
Rainbows beam out straight across the sky,
When the air turns cooler,
And the days grow darker,
The sweet aroma of autumn begins,
The hot beauty of the summer garden is no longer there,
Crunch, crunch, crunch feel the leaves underfoot,
And the howling of the wind streams through the door once again.

Harriet Toogood (12)
Great Torrington School

SCHOOL POEM

Monday morning at the bus stop,
Look around, got cereal on my top.
Get on the bus, find a front seat,
At the next stop, my best friend I meet.
Sat in class during registration
Waiting for the next lesson, in my imagination.
When the bell rings, people jump up,
Stand behind chairs, teacher says 'Shut up!'
Lunch is busy, pizzas are great,
At the dessert tray, full of cakes.
History next, oh what a bore,
Can't wait for the bell, to get out of the door.
Sit on the bus on my way back,
Tired and sleepy, it's the way I act.

Alice Brosnan-Guers (11)
Great Torrington School

THE JUNGLE

The deserted jungle lying all alone,
The trees are standing, some as thick as stone.
Animals are roaming, catching all their prey.
The jungle is haunted so some people say.

The jungle tribe live here too,
But the jungle is no place for me or for you.
Birds and mammals, creatures galore,
The jungle's so peaceful, I wish there was more.

Keith Bateman (12)
Great Torrington School

SEASONS

Spring is a time of joy,
flowers begin to bloom.
Fish spawn, leaves begin to grow
in different shades of green.

Summer, a hot time of the year,
leaves and flowers at their best.
Birds chirping all the time.
Beach packed all the time.

Autumn, the time of year when
leaves fall off in different shades of brown.
Birds leave the nest.
The wind picks up with a howl.

Winter, a cloak of white lying on the ground,
animals hibernating in the warmth.
Christmas on its way.
A fire blazing in your home.

Nicholas Hunt (12)
Great Torrington School

THE LIFE OF A SEAL

When they are young they have such soft fur,
They lie around and do not stir,
For them their mothers love and care.
With their pretty eyes they stare.

They grow older and larger,
and leave their homes,
and go off to start a family of their own.

Amy Anderson (12)
Great Torrington School

APPLES

Apples are very nice when they are ripe
crunchy, but good for you.
Some are red,
some are green,
some are even yellow.
Apples have stalks but they are not very strong,
they can be easily bruised.
If you leave them too long, they will go rotten
but if you don't they're OK.
They are not very big, nor very small, they are about medium-sized,
smooth on the outside.
crunchy on the inside.

But most of all they are healthy.

Benjamin Smart (11)
Great Torrington School

THE SEASONS

Winter comes and autumn goes
The snow sets in and the grass has disappeared
The autumn leaves fall as floating birds
Softly as the gentle breeze sets in
The small branches start to dance
As the wind slowly speeds
Soon
The winds blow so all the leaves are in the air
But really I don't care.

Dawn Ryan (11)
Great Torrington School

7:30AM

It's half-past seven
I'm still in bed
And thoughts of school
run round my head.

What day is it?
Have I got PE?
Do I need my books?
Have I got RE?
Where's my bag?
And my other shoe?
Have I got time
to go to the loo?
If I don't get going
I'll miss my bus
Why can't I leave
without this fuss?

Then it hits me
like a dazzling ray
I'm not going anywhere
Because it's *Saturday.*

Josh Catling (11)
Great Torrington School

STARTING SCHOOL

Starting school a new way,
Starting for the first day.
Everything seems to be new.
It's home time *phew!*

Ready for a new day.
Hang on a minute, I've lost my way.
I find myself in a year 10 class
I go all stiff like frozen glass.

Lunch time comes,
And I line up
Surrounded by boys, I wonder why.
Oh no! I'm in the wrong line.

I soon get used to a new school
Settle down, I'm just fine.
No more embarrassment
The day is through.

Gina Hocking (11)
Great Torrington School

WHAT A FOOL?

On my first day of primary school,
I made myself look a right old fool
It all started when our teacher, Mrs Ball,
Said 'Now, when I call your name say *yes Miss*,'
Well on and on and on went the names.
Then I recognised my own,
And by accident I shouted 'Yes Sir!'

Leitza Gorman (11)
Great Torrington School

HALLOWE'EN STEW

Witches, ghosts, vampires too,
all mixed up in my Hallowe'en stew.

The wildest costumes have sprung into life,
Frankenstein outfits with ripped trousers are rife.

People in groups of one or two, ready to jump out and shout *'Boo!'*
all mixed up to make my Hallowe'en stew.

Pumpkins with their glowing eyes,
Sit in house windows as a horrific surprise.

Fascinated people say *'Aah'* and *'ooh'*
as they see the outfits made out of goo.

They're all mixed up in my Hallowe'en stew!

Jay Whiting (11)
Great Torrington School

MOVING HER WAY THROUGH WATER

Moving her way through the water,
By her side her swimming daughter,
She's small now but is going to get bigger,
As she gets bigger her blubber gets thicker,
Gliding across the moving sea,
Trying to catch his prey for his family.

Amy Boyd (11)
Great Torrington School

AUTUMN MORNING

Dawn light filters over the treetops
Into the mist coloured valley.
The animals emerge.
A fox lopes across a frost-covered field
As a robin trills in the crisp morning air.
Squirrels gather nuts.
And hedgehogs snuffle in the loam
While leaves change their colours.

Dewdrops glisten on strands of silk
That makes up the spider's web.
On the farm a cock crows
And a buzzard circles lazily above a small copse
As the sun continues to rise.

Andrew J Robinson (12)
Great Torrington School

LEAF SEASONS

The small buds in spring,
So strong and full of youth,
The lush green leaves in summer,
Fully grown, big and matured,
Autumn turns them all colours,
And they become weak and brittle,
The transparent leaves of winter,
Dying, dying, dead.

Robin Judson (11)
Great Torrington School

SUMMERTIME

A hot summer's day
The sun drifting in the pure blue sky
Beautiful flowers all different colours
The sun was bright it made so much light
I took off my jumper
And sat in the shade
I felt cool and fresh
So I drank lemonade.

The breeze was passing across my face
I moved around at a lazy pace
All was quiet
Nobody was there
I felt alone
I felt aware
Trees were waving from side to side
I got on my bike and went for a ride.

Katie Elston (11)
Great Torrington School

THE BIG ONE

I sat beside the water
In the winter sunshine,
Waiting for the fish to jump.
It was nice and peaceful,
Until the big one took.
Then it was hard work to bring it in.
The prize was mine.

Alex Brine (11)
Great Torrington School

MONDAY MORNING FEVER

Thursday morning and up he gets,
Wiggles his toes and stretches his legs,
'Ah' he sighs and then he says,
'It's Thursday today.'

Friday morning and up he gets,
Wiggles his toes and stretches his legs,
Blinks his eyes, heaves a great sigh,
And then he says
'It's Friday today.'

Saturday morning and up he gets,
Wiggles his toes and stretches his legs,
Blinks his eyes,
Heaves a great sigh,
Makes his bed and then he says,
'It's Saturday today.'

Sunday morning up he gets,
Wiggles his toes and stretches his legs,
Blinks his eyes, heaves a great sigh
Makes his bed,
Bumps his head,
Then he says,
'It's Sunday today.'

Monday morning and up he gets,
Wiggles his toes, and stretches his legs,
Blinks his eyes,
Heaves a huge sigh, makes his bed,
Nods his head, and then he says,
'It's Monday, and I'm going back to bed.'

Jenny Le-Seelleur (11)
Great Torrington School

MY PUPPY

I wake up,
It's Saturday morning and only half-past seven.
I feel my face,
It's soaking wet,
She's woken me up again.
I look around to see where she's hiding,
And there at the bottom of my bed,
I see her little tail sticking out,
She's trying to hide under my quilt.
I try to be angry,
I promise you I do,
But I look into those big brown eyes,
And decide it's just no good.
She licks me with her warm wet tongue,
As if to say 'Oh thank you,
I promise I won't do it again,
At least until tomorrow.'

Sarah Ashton (11)
Great Torrington School

DOLPHINS

It is blue like the sky,
On a hot summer's day,
Moving through the water
Like an aeroplane dashing past,
Spraying water everywhere as it glides along.
Pointed fins and a gleaming smooth nose.
I am a dolphin and everybody knows.

Karis Craven-Wilkinson (11)
Great Torrington School

ALL ALONE

Here I am all alone,
In a corner on my own,
No one to talk to,
No one to see,
All the walls closing in on me.

Barricaded in a world of my own,
No one to take me into their home,
No one to comfort me,
No one who cares.

Deserted by my family who have all gone away,
Not even a rat has come out today
Dejected, deserted, unhappy and insecure,
No one in three days has knocked on the door.

Here I am all alone,
In a corner on my own,
No one to talk to,
No one to see,
I'm unhappy, unhappy as can be.

Kate Clements (12)
Great Torrington School

WAKING UP ON THE FARM

I wake to the sound of the cows mooing
over the deserted fields.
The morning dew glitters in the faint sun.
The tractor engine shakes the ground
like an earthquake.
My eyes, by then are wide awake.

Nicholas Bale (11)
Great Torrington School

RED

The red blood
Of the dangerous teacher
walking through the
alerted class
of terrified pupils
moving bags and boxes in her
path of destruction
she turns back
and braces
herself
for the attack.

Tom Williams (11)
Great Torrington School

THE MYSTERIOUS DOLPHIN

Way way down in the deep blue sea
A dolphin came and stared at me
With shining eyes and silver skin
We swam and played till the sun went in
Games of chase and hide and seek
Rolling and tumbling down in the deep
At last the day came to an end
Back amongst the other mermen
With a flick of his tail he was gone again.

Katy Greenslade (11)
Great Torrington School

SUMMER

Summer is light
Butterflies fly.
The sun is bright
in the sky.
Flowers are opening
during the day.
We're not joking
they open in May.
We're out in the garden
on our sunbed.
Dropping to sleep.
You sleepy head . . .

Debbie Elkins (11)
Great Torrington School

THE SUN

The sun shines bright,
In the light,
The sun is yellow,
Just like the stars at night,
In the night the sun sleeps,
When dawn comes,
The sun awakes,
To brighten up the day.

Samantha Headon (11)
Great Torrington School

To Treasure Always

The day skips through from dawn till dusk
the time has no importance.
You need to have dreams to make life true
Where will you be?
On the tropical breeze drifting off to paradise
The love of floating
the thought of the future
Something of someone to cherish
The bubbles from an icy crystal champagne glass
the deep red velvet drapes across my bed
a candlelit dinner
beautiful but sad
You don't know whether you've captured someone's heart.

Chloë Threadgould (12)
Great Torrington School

My Rabbit

I've just cleaned out my rabbit hutch,
A thing I hate to do!
It's not because I'm idle,
But it's something I must do!

My rabbit's name is Snowdrop,
I've had him quite some time.
But if he were to pass away,
I think I might just cry.

Dale Partridge (11)
Great Torrington School

MOON DANCER

Every night under the moon,
I see someone, somebody, something
dancing all alone, magically under
the moonbeam's spotlight.

As I stare through the window,
The moon dancer touches my heart,
Motionally gliding, drifting and
sweeping through the air.

On swift feet she twists and leaps, like a
Free spirit, unaware of the world around her.
Then without warning, she disappears
into the night sky, leaving me to wonder.

Jessica Day (11)
Great Torrington School

THE WOODLAND

Ivy climbing up the tree,
Toadstools round the base,
Pigeons flying fast and free,
Squirrels playing chase.

Doves are calling,
Sweet melodies are all around,
Acorns are falling,
What a wonderful sound.

Vicky Anderson (12)
Great Torrington School

WORLDS APART

Some countries have loads of food
which means they are well fed.
They have clean water
they have computers
they have a nice soft bed.

Though others aren't as lucky as that
people are hungry, starving.
With only dirty water to drink
they'd do anything for food
and a decent place to sleep.

That's why some people think
that they are worlds apart.

Ian Gilbert (14)
Great Torrington Schoo

COLDS

Sniffs and sneezes, coughs and flu,
Wrapped in bed, hot water bottle too.
Big red blanket over my head,
Don't wake me up, I think I'm dead.
My nose is blocked,
My throat is sore,
I think I'm going to *s-s-s-sneeze*
Once more.

Emma Heywood
Great Torrington School

KALEIDOSCOPE

Red and yellow, blue and green all these colours
can be seen.
Up and down, all around, different colours can be found.
Circles, triangles, rectangles and squares
you can see patterns as you glare.
Big and bold, bright and dull, patterns form
when you look in the hole.

Oliver Lulham (11)
Great Torrington School

HUMPTY'S RED CAR

Humpty Dumpty drove a red car.
Humpty Dumpty did not get far.
The breakdown lorry towed him away.
The little car is in the garage today.

Kerry Vanstone (12)
Great Torrington School

THE ZOO

In the zoo giraffes are very tall.
Rhinos are big. Tortoises crawl.
Zookeepers always working day and night.
Baboons' bums can give people an awful fright.

Lucy Kesseler (12)
Great Torrington School

ANGLING DREAMS

F ishing is my favourite hobby.
I go if and when I can.
S itting patiently by the waters.
H opeful dreams of catching a monster.
I f I do (I don't know if I ever will)!
N ever would I keep it, just return it back safely.
G o home again, no trophy, just the thrill.

I dream of striking lucky one day.
S tories and myths of giant catches.

F ifty pounds in weight and more through history.
U nder the surface, what lurks down there?
N ever shall I know, it remains a mystery.

Edward Haskins (13)
Great Torrington School

WHAT'S EXPECTED

Keep on the right hand side of the corridor.
This you can't ignore.
Do what the prefects say.
This you have to do every day.
Treat each other with respect.
That's what they all expect.
Sit on your chairs properly.
If only they had made them comfortably.
This is a little bit of what's expected although
everyone's tired of it it's not being rejected!

Andrea Reed (11)
Great Torrington School

THE KILLER WHALE

For a whale how wonderful it must be,
to go anywhere in the deep blue sea.
With the sky above
and the sea beneath,
he peacefully glides about the coral reef.
He swims so silent
you don't know he's there.
Until without warning he blows up for air.
With a size so huge
he has no fears
but he must beware when Man appears.
For Man is cruel - he does not care.
He will kill and kill and kill
until the sea is bare.

Sarah Jennings (12)
Great Torrington School

THERE WAS AN OLD BAKER WHO LIVED IN A MILL

There was an old baker who lived in a mill.
As far as I know he's making bread still.
He burnt his poor hand on a loaf of bread
his hand swelled up and went a pinky red.

He spent a week resting still in bed.
His hand so sore he was biting on lead.
While he was ill he was losing money
at this rate, his tea was bread and honey.

Ian Gilbert (12)
Great Torrington School

LITTLE AS LARGE

Cats and kittens
they are the world to me.
Babies mittens
little and sweet to see.

Big things come in small packages
small bubbles can make an almighty fizz.
A puppy looks sweet
when he's licking his feet.
Mum says 'Not when his gifts stain the floor!'

Kyla Manenti (12)
Great Torrington School

CHRISTMAS STAR

Christmas time and Christmas star
shining brightly from very far.
Christmas stories have been read
children cosy in their beds.

When they wake up
what will they see.
Presents piled high
all around the tree.

Lee K Holmes (12)
Great Torrington School

MAN U

Man U, Man U - what a team
they are just not what they seem.
Brilliant at football on the pitch
winning the matches without a hitch.
Man U, Man U - what a team
they are just a football dream.

Beckham, Cole and Neville too
Yorke and Scholes to add a few.
Shooting at the goal at the speed of light
playing to the end, putting up a fight.
Man U, Man U - what a team
they are just the best, *the cream* . . .

Ralph Atton (12)
Great Torrington School

SEASHORE

The sand as soft as snow,
the blue-green sea is shallow.
The sea breeze is light
the sun is bright
as I eat my marshmallow.

The night came fast
we were the last
to leave our heaven on earth.

Carly-Jo Daniels (12)
Great Torrington School

EEL

Eel
what a creep.
His slimy skin
his long tail.
He is oh so strong.
What is giving off that awful pong?
He's grabbed my arm.
He won't let go.
You feel his pulse - but it is so slow.
He is so so cold.
Eel - he has a hold on my arm.
You can't get it off.
Or so I'm told!

Michael Day (13)
Great Torrington School

MY HAMSTER

My hamster whirls round and round
on his miniature merry-go-round.

He munches nuts and slurps his water.
My hamster.

The wriggles and twitches are because of his itches,
he's fluffy and fat but most of all he's
My hamster.

Louise Bond (12)
Great Torrington School

RITUAL PATIENCE

Lie still
Watch
Watch them scramble
Watch the dust fly
They are wary
But they bend to drink
Sense takes over
And they bolt
Scanning the surface with huge eyes
No!
Don't leave!
They will be back
Remember
They are thirsty.

Matthew Grainger (13)
Great Torrington School

DINOSAURS

Dinos, Dinos
everywhere around me.
They're eating me,
tearing me.

It's going to hurt
be unbearable.
They're chomping away
digesting poor me!

James Norris (12)
Great Torrington School

THE LION'S TERRITORY

The anger in his eyes as a second lion walks in
on his territory.
He looks and stares to make everyone know
that he is the ruler.
King of the jungle.
The lions walk towards each other, both of them
up for a fight.
Silence . . . then suddenly
Roar! The fight begins.
The claw that scratches, the teeth that gnaw.
Just like the street gangs, keeping people off
their turf.
The proudness as the second lion yelps
and runs off into the distance.
The king is once again supreme.

Louise Headon (14)
Great Torrington School

WINTER

Snow is falling
from up in the sky.
It is softly floating by.

Rain is coming
winter is here.
Gales are blowing
from year to year.

Hannah Stanley
Great Torrington School

THE CROWD

All tight black hipsters, glossy lips, dyed hair.
She spots this crowd. She wants to be there.
A group of twenty, maybe less or more.
She would have to pass their entry law.
Faces stare as she approaches the crowd,
She looks for warmth in their eyes; but cold.
They study her closely as she says her name,
She wants to be accepted. Be brave and bold.

Stealing from the local newsagents was easy.
She was really beginning to fit right in.
Twenty pounds from her mother's purse was easy,
Shared a cigarette, a beer, baked beans from a tin.
Like a raindrop from the sky, she did as she was told.
Get drunk, was stupid, did wrong, felt great.
She was now a piece in the picture, a part of the crowd.
She had new friends, but was too blind to see her fate.
Gradually, the fly was stuck in the web.
The spiders had grabbed her and made her theirs.
They had a new hobby, a craze that would last.
Make them high, with a boost and a blast.
Drugs were powerful and easy to get,
Used daily, their magic was met.
She was scared of their new-found joy,
But loneliness is hard to bear, so shared hers with a boy.

She was not a lucky girl. Dead in the morning.
Hospital first.
Lost her life to be with the crowd.
The crowd that was supposed to be her every dream.
The crowd that was 'in' and big, and powerful.
The crowd that laughed no more . . .

Tannaze Tinati (16)
Great Torrington School

THE OWL

The wise old owl
sits high in the tree.
Waiting for some unexpected
rodent to pass by.
The clever wise owl waits
and then the patient owl swoops
and snatches the vole.
The diligent owl has won his supper.

Rachel Knight (13)
Great Torrington School

SUMMERTIME

Summertime is here again
children playing in their den.
Journey's from the east and west
birds are laying in their nest.
Now the summer is long gone
I hope nothing will go wrong.

Abigail Worth (12)
Great Torrington School

SUMMER

Cheerful nice
swimming, running, sunbathing,
beach, sand, rain, snow.
Sleighing, snow-boarding, snowballing.
Cold icy.
Winter.

Lance Appleton (14)
Great Torrington School

A WISE OLD OWL

A wise old owl sees its prey
it swoops down and snatches it up.
Like we would a chocolate bar on the floor.
He hears a cat,
he'd better get out of the way
or he might end up as the prey.
But the owl is too wise, he flies back
to his nest.
For a long days rest.
Wise old owl!

Kyle Warrington (14)
Great Torrington School

THE CHEETAH

It's very fast and swift
and has a watchful eye.
It swiftly moves across the land
and spots its prey up ahead.
Suddenly it all turns to greed.
Then nothing stands in its way
except its dinner.
It pounces and chokes it by the neck
and the gracefulness turned to roughness.

Lisa Harper (13)
Great Torrington School

THE LAVA

The lava spills
ready to pop.
Nearly there
getting closer
then . . .
Bang it goes
coming closer
down the hill.
People running fast
they don't look back.
They are safe,
watching the village
and nothing reappeared.

Lee Cockwill (11)
Great Torrington School

RABBIT

Ears to the ground
listening for the slightest sound.
It hears a sound, it starts to run.
Quickly, quietly, cowardly it runs.
It starts to get faster, faster.
Quickening with fright at this terrible sight.
It slows, it's gone.
It turns the corner.
Only to be a mourner.

Karl Curtis (13)
Great Torrington School

THE SUN

I look up into the sky
I see the sun so high.
You could not buy anything more
to keep us warm and dry.
If it was not there, we would
surely die.

At night I see the stars so bright
but not at such might
as our sun in full flight.
It's on by day and out by night
and keeps on staying nice and
bright.

Ben Jenkinson (12)
Great Torrington School

THE YO-YO

It's the latest craze everyone likes.
It's fun, it's fab, it's full of challenge.
It's good and everyone wants one.
With the skill of the hand and the
flick of the wrist.
The Yo-Yo world is in the mist.
Everyone is trying to learn new tricks.
With the Yo-Yo gang it's all a big mix.
All the time they're trying their best
because they all want to beat the rest.

Jamie Ellis (12)
Great Torrington School

7 AGES OF MAN

A young soldier
fighting for his team.
Full of armour
and looks very keen.
The soldier awaits
to hear the signal and bang!
They're off!
All you hear
is a scream and a charge.
A minute to go
and over 2000 people
are dead and now
it's all over and they are
cheering after winning
the fight.

Adam Vanstone (12)
Great Torrington School

FOOTBALL

You get Michael Owen
with the speed.
Robbie Fowler with
the feet.
Steve Macmanaman with the
need to score another goal.
Liverpool have it all
when it comes to
football.

Dane Jenkins (13)
Great Torrington School

THE MOONWALK

'One small step for man'
that's what I said.
'One giant leap for mankind.'
that's what I said.
Can you guess who I am?
I'm the man on the moon
that's who I am.
Moon, moon, I am over the moon.
To actually step upon the moon.
Now can you guess who I am?
I'm sure you will guess very soon.
Beep! Beep! 'Moon to Earth.
Come in Earth, come in quick.'
I am standing on the moon
it feels all floaty.
It doesn't feel real.
My word, it's mad!
There's no way to describe it.
It's like a dream.
It's like I have gone to heaven unseen.
Now I bet you have guessed who I am!
Neil Armstrong . . . that's who I am.

Matthew A Phillips (12)
Great Torrington School

A REALLY BORING POEM

Miss said to write a poem,
but I don't know where to start.
Miss said it's really easy,
but I think that it's an art.

I think they're really boring.
I can't write them at all.
I wish I could write a poem.
That was really, really cool.

I'd write about some dragons
and damsels in distress.
But I know that if I started,
I'd end up in a mess.

I can't think of a thing,
Words go in and out my head.
Forget the silly poem,
I'll go and play instead.

Tim Judson (12)
Great Torrington School

CHRISTMAS TIME

It's 25th December
the time to remember.
The day Jesus was born.
We celebrate with turkey and stuffing.
The tree shines bright
with fairy lights . . .

Felicity Reid (12)
Great Torrington School

THE BIG ISSUE

I am homeless, I have nowhere to go.
I sell the Big Issue, people say 'No!'
I sit on the street with nothing to eat.
All I really want is a nice comfortable seat.
I stand there with the Big Issue in hand
Other people think they're so grand.
I've been standing here for 5 hours with nothing to do.

Guess how many I've sold - 2!
I think I'll give up now with my one pound twenty.
That won't buy me plenty.
People stop and stare at me.
They laugh and point at me.
I feel so lonely and empty inside
No one would really care if I died.
I feel so sad - I want to die.
Then I'd be kissing the world goodbye.
Because all I really am is a Big Issue seller.
A stupid smelly - homeless old begger.

Sarah Payne (12)
Great Torrington School

I HAVE A ZOO

I have a zoo
All to myself
I keep it in my room
And under the hallway shelf

I keep a giraffe in my cupboard
A lion on my chair
A tiger under my desk
And a gorilla on my bed

I have a zoo
All to myself
I keep it in my room
And under the hallway shelf.

Lauren Hildebrand (13)
Hele's School

THE HOLIDAY

The sea laps gently on the sand
A cool breeze drifts across the wide blue ocean
The silent glint of the sun makes the water look mirror-like
The golden sand stands untouched in the morning stillness

Surfers strut down the beach
Children with inflatables hurry through the rock pools
Parents sunbathe and watch the kiddies play
Sun cream and ice-cream, and laughing with friends

Sipping red wine at the Sunset Bar
Watching the day unfold
Views of yachts and headlands and flowers
Hotels filled with tourists, bustling town below

Exploring a new cave, excitement as you enter the dark place
Buckets filled with shells, sandcastles and beach balls
Bodyboards and surfboards, wetsuits and swimsuits
Having a great time

Walking, weeping on your last day
Sunset forms an amazing show of deep red and purple
Last waves crash onto the rocks
Another year over, another year to come.

Rachel Knight (13)
Hele's School

THE SEA

Beneath the winter night's sky
Lay the sea,
Shimmering in the silver moonlight.
It lay still,
Not a movement in sight, but
The waves gently lapping on the shore.

But in the depths of the ocean,
The clear water is filled with movement,
A thousand fish dart around beneath the surface,
Between the seaweed and coral.

Back at the shore,
I stand staring and wondering,
How deep is the sea? And
How far does it go?
A million thoughts rush through my mind,
As I stand there beside
The sea!

Joanne Greer (12)
Hele's School

LOVE

When you are down
And feeling blue
I'll be there
To comfort you.

Please don't cry
I'll stay here
To bring you love
No need to fear.

I'll give you good loving
All through the night
Please don't worry baby
I'll do you right

I'll stay here forever
I'll never let you go
Please don't leave without me
Because I love you so.

Mo Fawzi (12)
Hele's School

FLYING THROUGH THE AIR

Arrive in the air
At ten thousand feet
Very lonely
No one to meet
Float to jump into the air
Come on mate, this can't be fair!
Don't make me do this
I can't jump out of there.
I look down into the gloom
Thinking when the time will loom.
We jump out with a thrill
Then we see our landing hill
Suddenly we had landed,
Then we found we were stranded
On an island
No one to see
Please come and *rescue me!*

Dominic Wood (12)
Hele's School

FLUTE

How softly does the song play
A flute, high and low noted.
'A metal piece of junk,' some say.
They all prefer guitars
Not me though.
I prefer classical to heavy metal.
The flute
For spring, summer, autumn and winter tunes
The faint breeze, the nightingale, the midnight feast,
for happy or sad moments.

A love song, a walk, a marching band
The flute can play all those.
A leader in an orchestra
You play it with both hands.

Flute!

Alison Berrisford (12)
Hele's School

CHRISTMAS

Christmas is near
Don't shed a tear
Presents are coming at the end of each year.

Time for mince pies and Christmas cake
You better eat it now
Before it's too late!

Presents are given
Cards are sent
It's all about Jesus at this time of Advent.

Sarah Davis (12)
Hele's School

YO-YO PRO-YO

Yo-yo Pro-yo
Flying up and down
Yo-yo Pro-yo
Spinning all around.

Yo-yo Pro-yo
Zooming in the air
Yo-yo Pro-yo
Spinning everywhere

Yo-yo Pro-yo
Doing all the tricks
Yo-yo Pro-yo
Tosses and flicks

Yo-yo Pro-yo
Into rock the cradle
Yo-yo Pro-yo
Don't hit the table

Yo-yo Pro-yo
Strings in a knot
Yo-yo Pro-yo
Clutch is getting hot

Yo-yo Pro-yo
What a bad luck stroke
On no, Pro-yo
Yo-yo's *broke!*

Laurie Borlace (12)
Hele's School

MONOPOLY!

My brother and I play Monopoly,
He always cheats, then wins!
He never goes to jail,
But visits when I'm in.

Once he bought Vine Street
And I had to pay sixteen pounds if I landed on it,
Then he bought Mayfair and I thought
'Time to quit!'

But today I'm the banker,
It'll be me who cheats,
I'll give him what for!
He won't forget it for weeks!

Two hundred pounds you collect
When you pass 'Go'
To even the score
I collected more!

I bought Old Kent Road and Whitechapel,
Which he thought was funny,
With hotels on
He had to part with his money.

Chris threw a seven,
Pass 'Go' he went,
Two hundred pounds were his,
But that was soon spent.

He landed on Old Kent Road
For the second time,
Four hundred and fifty pounds, the rent,
Now the game was

Mine!

Kimberley Moses (12)
Hele's School

AUTUMN COLOURS

Autumn has arrived, and all around,
The leaves left on the trees are brown,
And all the rest have fallen down.

The rain falls harder, the sky turns grey,
There is not much light left in the day.

The sea turns dark, more grey than blue,
As it gets colder, there are less things outside to do.

It's winter now, the sky turns black,
Presents are here, already in the shed, out the back.

Winter's gone and spring is here,
The sheep give birth, the birds all cheer.

Summer's now here, but is almost gone,
The leaves will fall off the trees.
The sunny days will go, it won't be long.

Tracy Pengelly (12)
Hele's School

THE KNOCKOUT

I'll pound him, I'll crush him
I'll show him who's boss,
It will take me ten seconds to flatten him.

A right jab, a left jab, a punch in the stomach,
I'll uppercut him in the face.
I'll make his face go black and blue.

When he hits the mat,
I'll hear the ref count,
One, two, three, four, five, six,
Seven, eight, nine, ten,
Then I hear the bell,
I'm the winner of the match,
The deadly destructor.

Chris Smyth (12)
Hele's School

SPLAT!

Space, space, what an empty place you might think . . .
But with asteroids, planets and rockets galore
Space, space is a cosmic place
An alien 3-foot tall with thirty eyes but they're very small
With five noses all it does is snore!
The snore beast slowly slops its way with no legs
it's here to stay.
The snore beast crawls its way in a rocket,
blasts off and hits a
Comet!

Daniel Johnson (12)
Hele's School

THE SEA

The sea, the sea.
It's never still, always moving
Like blue jelly with foam on top.
Dolphins fly through the ocean
So fast and playful, they jump then
Splash!
Courageously the dolphins leap into the ocean.
The conflict starts between the waves.
It turns grey and the rain pours down
The sea now left
Like a cat licking up milk
So gracefully.

Leigh Curran (12)
Hele's School

AUTUMN

Autumn season has come once again
With its colder nights and darker evenings
Conkers begin to fall from the trees
Then they crack open, ripe and ready
For us to collect.
This really is my favourite time of year
Standing underneath the trees
And watching the dry crunchy leaves
Flutter down around me.
Gold, red, orange, brown
A sea of colours all around.

Brooke Edgecombe (12)
Hele's School

KALEIDOSCOPE

Looking through a kaleidoscope
See winter with just one eye,
It is so amazing.
See colours of winter leaves
Red, yellow, orange and brown
Is that amazing too?

Turning round the kaleidoscope
I see spring
Popping out of tiny buds
yellow, pink, red and green
Little flower, little buds
Appearing from nowhere.

Now turning for the last time
Start the poem again
And see how amazing
That is for
You!

Sophie Lock (11)
Hele's School

KALEIDOSCOPE OF COLOURS

Fireworks lighting up the sky
Rockets shooting way up high
Beautiful colours overhead
Yellow, green, blue and red
Sparklers held very tight
Writing letters big and bright
The bonfire is glowing hot
Catherine wheels spin on the spot.

Adam Frame (11)
Hele's School

128

KALEIDOSCOPE

Green and brown, the colours of trees.
Orange and blue, are the colours for me.
Black and yellow make a bumblebee,
Tiny black dots - the itchy fleas.

Grey is the colour of growing old.
A peachy head, might mean you're bald!
White long posts for scoring a goal,
Purple bruises the result of a foul.

All sorts of colours make the world
Which means they are the best,
But probably the best of all is . . . *gold*
Of course, *yes!*

Gary Downes (12)
Hele's School

THE WHISPERS OF THE OCEAN

The seagulls cry, the tumblers roll,
And I see all this as I go for my stroll.
I pick up a shell and place it by my ear,
And all the whispers of the ocean I can hear.
A feeling of excitement as the water touches my toes,
This is a feeling that nobody else knows.
I can feel the breeze on my skin,
As the tide of the ocean rushes in.
As I walked back towards my house,
A dolphin I spotted with its lifelong spouse.

Kelsey Leather (11)
Hele's School

KALEIDOSCOPE

My kaleidoscope looks like little beads
that are trying to escape.

The beads twist,
The beads twirl
and bang around inside,
but then the kaleidoscope rests again
you can't bring back what's gone.

A kaleidoscope is a funny thing
it reminds me of trees,
when all the leaves fall and rustle around in the wind.
A kaleidoscope reminds me of lots of things.
Does it seem strange to you?

Sheryl Wood (11)
Hele's School

LEAVES

Brown, yellow, green, orange,
these are the colours
of the leaves.
See them falling in the air
falling, falling
everywhere.
See them floating so
gentle and calm
they look like little
spaceships.

Ben Ackrell (11)
Hele's School

BONFIRE NIGHT

My birthday is on this day,
The day Guy Fawkes gets burnt.
And I have learned not to get burnt
And I have learnt my lesson.
Fireworks going off and off and never stopping.
Where do they go?
The bonfire is lit to keep us warm,
But there's one thing!
What's that?
We are in our English form.

Michelle Russell (11)
Hele's School

KALEIDOSCOPE

Oranges, yellows, reds and browns
Are the colours of the autumn leaves

Falling lightly on the ground
As a sheet of leaves forms

As the autumn begins to end
Green buds appear on the trees

Then green leaves appear
Yet again for another year.

Sarah Lake (11)
Hele's School

MY OLDER BROTHER

My older brother is football crazy,
He doesn't get up, he is very lazy.
He likes to go out and play with his mate,
He doesn't come home. He is often late.
He supports Man U and Plymouth Argyle,
But he hasn't been to see them for a while.
He never has a bath and doesn't wash,
And he always seems to have lots of dosh.
he goes to bed and snores loudly all night,
In the morning he looks an awful sight!

Becky McDonnell (11)
Hele's School

THE GARDEN GNOME

In my garden, there is a happy gnome
He likes to fish and clean out his home.
He loves to fish for minnows for his dish
He doesn't like to catch many other fish.
Bright yellow boots he wears on his small feet,
His sou'wester has buttons that don't meet.
A bright red cap sits on his weathered head,
And 'Begara and Bejabers!' he's said.
He has many colourful happy friends,
And now my poem is going to end.

Paula Anderson (11)
Hele's School

THE TEST

I wake up in the morning ready for the test.
I get up, get my pants on, I almost forget my vest.
I'm coming down the stairs and I need to brush my hair.
It sticks up like a lamp post but it's lovely, blonde and fair.
I'm hungry for my breakfast and some coffee and some tea,
But first before I leave now, I must just go for a wee.
I get on my new coat and grab a piece of toast,
My book of English grammar is halfway down my throat.
The test's about to start now, and I have a throbbing heart.
My work on English grammar is worse than a scary shark.
I have not got a pencil or a pen to start me off,
A girl sits in the corner, they call her 'The Boff'.
I'm halfway through the test now and I'm thinking this is hard.
I'm still on question 1, but it's on the second half.
The test is almost over and I'm glad it's been and gone
But I'd better start to run now or I'm going to miss the bus.

Amy Berrisford (11)
Hele's School

MY MUM

Whenever I feel ill my mum may give me a pill.
When I'm feeling sad she'll say 'Don't feel bad.'
The days I'm in a muddle I know she'll always
                                    give me a cuddle.
But if my mum needed me by her side I know she
                                    has her pride,
I would be as she is with me and help as much as need be.
Because she is my mum and can be great fun,
I will respect and love her second to none.

Sophie Theophilus (11)
Hele's School

FIRST DAY AT HELE'S SCHOOL

First day at Hele's I never thought I would
Be able to do work, but after I felt good.

In all my life I don't believe
That a school could be as big as this.

For lunch I had lovely things
What I wished for was what God brings.

At the end of the day I'm as happy as can be.

I like school, it's as wonderful as can be,
But sometimes it's as boring as can be.

Tracy Ward (11)
Hele's School

ORPHANS AROUND THE WORLD

Some children abroad are very alone,
Some are very ill and scared and have no homes.

Sleeping in the horrible conditions,
They are skinny and malnutritioned.

From babies to adults live in these homes
They wish they could find a nice, happy home.

I hope this poem makes you understand
That people in this world need *a helping hand.*

Laura Heard (11)
Hele's School

THE BOXER

I am a boxer
As you can see
I am a boxer
Yes, that's me

I am so strong
I am the best
I lost to Tyson
But won all the rest

If you fight me
You're bound to lose
I would even beat you
During a snooze.

James Bailey (11)
Hele's School

SCHOOL

Children running everywhere,
Classes full, none are bare.
Assemblies taken in the hall,
Waiting for the bell to call.
Outdoor lessons on the grass,
Teachers saying 'Quiet class!'
PE lessons with a ball and bat
Someone's brought in a pet cat!
I go to school every day and
Enjoy whatever comes my way.

Samantha MacDougall (11)
Hele's School

OLD

I'm old and wrinkled,
I'm down in the dumps,
I stay in bed,
And have big lumps.

I never get out of bed
Because of my swollen head,
I can't walk an inch,
Out of my bed.

I wish I'd never climbed that tree,
And fallen on my head,
If I'd never climbed that tree,
I wouldn't be in this bed.

I wear funny glasses,
I'm shivering and cold,
I wear a wig,
Because I'm bald!

Marc O'Leary (12)
Hele's School

MY NEXT DOOR NEIGHBOUR

My next door neighbour is wrinkly and old
He needs a stick to walk down the road.
He wears lots of clothes but he still gets a cold.
I don't really want to get old.

He rants and he raves at my brother and me
Especially when we make a noise
While he's drinking his tea.
It's my brother who makes the noise,
But he always blames me.

He likes to do lots of gardening
To keep him nice and busy
He likes to grow flowers especially busy Lizzies
I don't want to grow old.

Natalie Harris (11)
Hele's School

THE DOLPHIN

The sparkly reflection
From the deep blue sky,
The sea on fire
From the setting sun,
The waves crashing on
The rocks, glistening,
Like frothy shaken lemonade.

Dolphins arching over the waves,
Over the sunset,
Like arrows shooting to the sun.

The sea no longer sparkles blue,
But black as midnight,
The oil slicks sliding
Glistening,
Under the silver moon.

A solitary dolphin
Washed up on the shore,
Still. No breath. No life. Helpless.

Alix Triscott (11)
Hele's School

A HALLOWE'EN CHILL OF LAUGHTER

Witches, witches, in the air
Flying above your heads
'Please Sir
Please Sir
Have you a bob or two?'
Children scurrying amongst
The streets
Like little tiny rats
Knock, knock
Knock
Echoing through the streets
And children's
Screams of laughter
And mums saying
'Stay in the street
Don't go far
Or else!
And don't go knocking
On the old lady's
Door -
You will get
A big smack!
So be warned!'

Roxanne Piper (11)
Hele's School

HALLOWE'EN

Hallowe'en is drawing near,
Everyone gives a frightening cheer.
This is the night when ghouls come out,
Ghosts and zombies give a fearful shout.
People dress up in funny clothes, as ghosts,
Zombies, vampires and witches on broomsticks.
Trick or treating, sweets and more, toffee apples,
I can't eat anymore.
Help! A mummy,
Got to run!
Hallows Eve's just a bit of fun.
31st October is the fun and fearful night.
This night gives people frights.
Hallowe'en is one of the best nights.

Matthew Fittock (11)
Hele's School

BONFIRE NIGHT

Bonfire burning brightly
Guy Fawkes sitting sadly on the sensational bonfire,
Fireworks flying furiously,
Rockets racing in the sky.
Catherine wheels spinning and sparking,
Staring skywards, searching for
Shimmering splashes of colour.
Booming bangs burst everywhere,
Sending showers of colourful creations.

Daryoush Toorneini (11)
Hele's School

THE MAN

People often wonder why I sit here,
But when you think about it, it's quite clear.
I sit here every day wondering when I'll get my pay
Thinking who to spend it on
Perhaps I'll give it away.
My mother always thought I was a nice lad,
Even though I was really bad.
I'm a serious chap,
Hands resting on my lap.
It's hard to think I'm in a city.
The parks and gardens are so pretty.
I'll sit here a while longer,
Until my legs feel stronger.
Busy people rushing by
They don't have time to say 'Hi!'

Chloé Bawden (12)
Hele's School

TITANIC

As the Titanic sets sail people cheer and shout
Flags are waved and the band plays
The ship's horn sounds as loud as thunder.
The engines and boilers gear into action.
Thud, clang and hooray, it's sail time!

As the Titanic sinks, the band plays sadly
as something good is coming to an end.
Cries of 'Women and children first' and
'It's every man for himself' are heard
above the chaos as the deep dark waters
swallow the ship to the sand below.

As the Titanic is explored, pictures, ornaments
and clothes are found
It is as if time has been frozen.
Fish swim in the kitchens and seaweed
grows on the bed.

This is the life of the Titanic.

Elizabeth Stewart (11)
Hele's School

HALLOWE'EN

On the night of Hallowe'en,
The witches come and make you scream.
The devil comes and wakes you up,
Then he makes you drink a cup of blood.

On the night of Hallowe'en,
People dress up to make you scream.
They terrify the neighbourhood blood,
Hoping they will have some tasty food.

On the night of Hallowe'en,
The ghosts jump out and make you shout,
And Dracula comes to take a peep,
To see if you are fast asleep.

On the night of Hallowe'en,
The flying witches make you scream.
They fill you up with lots of fear,
And tell you they'll be back next year.

Toni Page (11)
Hele's School

A TRIBE

Just a tribe of us
all alone in the dust
On a wild African plain
people say we are insane
But we have our own good ways
and we get through all our days
Just a tribe of us
all alone in the dust

And we dance and we sing
round a bonfire to our king
The leader has a horn
he was blessed when he was born
His father taught him so
no one else will ever know
And we dance and we sing
round a bonfire to our king

In the misty night
you can hear them when they fight
They're out there on their own
but we know we're not alone
They will kill for their pride
you can see it in their stride
In the misty night
you can hear them when they fight.

Nick Frettsome (13)
Hele's School

A FRIEND I LOST

Such a short life, such a long day
The day my friend died
Her blue sapphire eyes no longer
Her curly blonde hair no more,
Her cute little smile which peered
through the door,
A cheerful cuddle in the morn.

A child, no more, came to her fate
The day I lost a mate
Her blue sapphire eyes no longer,
Her curly blonde hair no more,
Her cute little smile which peered
through the door,
A cheerful cuddle in the morn.

She ran across, all my fault,
I should have been there to hold her.
Her blue sapphire eyes no longer,
Her curly blonde hair no more,
Her cute little smile which peered
through the door,
A cheerful cuddle in the morn.

Victoria Bevan (12)
Hele's School

HALLOWE'EN IS HERE

Hallowe'en is here,
Ghosts, wolves and vampires galore.
Trick or treaters at your door.
Witches on broomsticks
And goblins come out.
They will make you run,
Make you scream,
Make you shout.
Pumpkins about, lighting the street,
Lots of yummy things to eat,
At the Hallowe'en party,
Everyone's there,
To give you a scare!
Zombies are here,
With their ghostie friends
As soon as you see them
You'll go round the bend.
When Hallowe'en's over
And everything's clear,
Now we look forward,
To Hallowe'en next year.

Jonathan Mottram (11)
Hele's School

PLEASE MUM, DON'T HAVE ANOTHER KID

I only have one pet brother
And I do not wish to have another
He steals my sweets and eats and eats.
He pulled the head of my favourite dolly off.
I was only two at the time.

We grew up together, still having war,
When he was six and I was four,
My mum came in with a big tummy
She said to us 'Listen kids,'
And my brother and I ran upstairs screaming!

Eleanor Sinclair (11)
Hele's School

MY RABBIT THINKS SHE'S A DOG

My rabbit is called Sabrina and she thinks she's a dog.
Fur as soft as a new-born baby's head,
My rabbit thinks she's a Rottweiler,
Eyes the colour of rich, dark chocolate,
My rabbit thinks she's a Rottweiler,
Body the colour of snow, with a muddy stripe,
Running straight down her back and spots either side,
My rabbit thinks she's a Rottweiler,
She hops merrily around the garden and in and out of the house.
My rabbit thinks she's a Rottweiler.
She lies and listens to the music,
She sits and watches TV.
My rabbit thinks she's a Rottweiler,
She lies by the fire like a sleepy dog,
My rabbit thinks she's a Rottweiler,
And why? you ask . . . *nip . . . ouch!*
She chases us around the garden,
Biting and nipping our ankles,
My Rabbit thinks she's a Rottweiler,
Her name is Sabrina,
She thinks she's a dog.

Victoria Roberts (11)
Hele's School

HORSE RIDING

There was a man riding a horse
Learning how to do a course
Jumping high off the ground
Going fast, round and round.
The horse went too fast
And tripped over a fence
Bad luck it was because
He broke his right leg,
He went to hospital
Which was two miles away
He was told to rest
And go there another day
A week later
He had gone horse riding again
He was in a competition
With three other men
They started the race
And he jumped the first fence
Number 11 was winning
But 12 overtook
Bad luck to the man
He still has more chances
If he tries his best, he will win against the rest.

Carly Stephens (12)
Hele's School

EYES IN DISGUISE

Why you ask, can we see?
Why isn't the world blank?
Full of blackness, darkness and mourning
Sat underwater . . . sank

Oh why don't we just sit around
Without any sight
Lonely and cold,
And hidden from the light?

Samantha Giffard (13)
Hele's School

AUSTRALIA

I held it for a minute
It gripped me
Cuddled me
Pressed his chest against mine
I was nervous
But then I wasn't
It had small spiky ears
It had sad eyes
It was furry
Spiky
Cute
I put his head on mine
It dug me
Scratched me
It was cute
I wanted it
I would have taken it right then
Then I let go
I loved it
It was a koala.

Sarah Woodley (12)
Hele's School

POUNCING CAT

Twitching and yawning the cat slowly wakes up
Out of the corner of his eye he sees something
Scurrying round in the corner.

What could it be?
Is it one of the children's toys?
Or a sock that has fallen from the washing basket?

Then he sees
It is a mouse
Small, grey, with long whiskers and a thin tail.

The cat lies silently
Staring at the mouse
Always keeping it in sight.

Slowly and carefully he gets ready to pounce
The mouse unaware still scurrying on,
While the cat leans back.

Miaow!
The cat pounces
The mouse is trapped.

It squeaks as loudly as it possibly can
Its attempts are useless
And the mouse catches its final glimpse of day.

Alison Tozer (12)
Hele's School

CHRISTMAS POEM

Travelling on the dusty road
Donkey carrying the heavy load.

Being carried over stones and rocks
Bumping the baby and giving him knocks.

This was a special baby and he was due
But his mother didn't know that, she didn't have a clue.

When they arrived in Bethlehem
It was crowded with women and lots of men.

They tried everywhere but there was nowhere to stay
Then Mary spotted a stable of hay.

And that was where they stayed for the night
But suddenly came a terrible fright.

The baby was born, he had come out
Then a wise man gave an excited shout.

He said 'We've found them and there they are
We've come a long way. We've followed the star.'

Then a young man came running like a bull
With his legs stampeding and his arms full.

In his arms he carried a sheep
And it gave a gentle, quiet bleat.

In a crib lay the quiet boy
Not making a sound, just a small smile of joy.

Carl Palmer (12)
Hele's School

SAVE THE RAINFOREST

Trees, trees, ever-lasting trees being cut down by chainsaws.
Monkeys screaming as their rainforest is going fast.
Lorries driving away with the wood,
Just to make charcoal for their factories.

Fish getting polluted and jumping out of the water.
Animals dying, it looks like they will never survive.
Snakes still slither looking for the bravest prey
Then it strikes!
And he swallows a mouse in one.

The birds start chirping,
They can see a forest fire heading this way.
The monkeys pass the message on,
And the area gets cleared just in time.

This is just an example of what they have to do to survive.
But we rely on the animals,
As well as the plants for food
Even though the scientists could create them in the future,
They would not be the same.

So we could help the animals, keep them alive,
If we act now and work together we have a chance to save the forest,
And everything in it!

Gary Menzies (12)
Hele's School

BIRDS OF PARADISE

Birds flying through the air,
No worries to scare,
To spoil their beautiful looks.

Their wings cut and tear.
The blue sky that is theirs from the start of time,
This is true paradise.

To be free to fly and dive.
All this for the birds of paradise.
For them it is good to be alive.

To be the birds of paradise,
To hop and fly,
To perch on a twig.

This is true paradise, this is not a lie.
To fly higher than the sun or the moon.
To have a home the size of a forest.

To soar in the air.
To own his adventure that we call life,
To avoid death by a wing.
But he is not happy, he has no friends.
He is alone.

Matthew Harris (12)
Hele's School

THE BOAT PEOPLE

Every day I return from work,
To the place I rest my head.
Relax, sit down, watch some TV,
Safe in the embrace of my daily bread.

My money that liberates,
My money that binds
My western life and me,
My so called 'Daily grind'.

Once upon a time I dreamt.
Once, before the world moved in
And forced its grey walls around my life.
Once, when I thought I could win.

I want to sail away,
I've just got to be free.
I need to run with the boat people
To escape my blue reality.

Just to be aboard the ship,
Just to sail into the dawn.
Just to escape our civil submission,
Not to bow, and scrape, and fawn.

Life no longer holds them back,
Their hearts and souls are free.
They sailed away to nowhere,
And found their destiny.

Jacob Rollinson (13)
Hele's School

WHAT'S BEHIND THOSE DOORS?

I wonder what's behind those doors
My imagination wanders.
A giant emerald forest full of wild boars
Or a raging storm which thunders.
People eating, dancing merry
Drinking sweet champagne or sherry
Gliding fast on a ferry,
Oh what's behind those doors.

I wonder what's behind those doors
My imagination wanders.
A sea of sapphire and golden shores
With pirates there to plunder.
Lots of creatures with good cheer
Never think of hate nor fear
Forever laughing, forbidden tear,
Oh what's behind those doors.

I wonder what's behind those doors
With guards standing yonder,
Large dark rooms, blood stained floors
People falling under.
Dare they talk of good and fun
Covering under naked gun
Can't escape so do not run,
I know what's behind those doors.

Luke Sloan (13)
Hele's School

THE TRAMP

Sitting alone in a doorway,
So hungry, dirty and cold.
Begging for hours for money,
His cardboard box covered in mould.

The refuge tries to help him,
Soup kitchens feed him more food.
The working people ignore his plight,
When they see him they are always rude.

Everyone hates and despises him.
But is it right for them to do so?
What would it be like to lose their homes?
And be told to get out and go?

Alexandra Marshall (13)
Hele's School

SHOES

I'm getting my first ballet shoes
the problem is which pair?
The colour of them has to match
the dress I'm going to wear.

I don't know which pair will fit me
the big ones or the small?
Which pair do I really want?
I don't know at all.

The shoe lady is really helpful
I'm having lots of fun
I can't wait till Mummy sees me
dancing in the sun.

Michelle Wilkins (13)
Hele's School

My Life

As I look at my village I think what a state,
It once was my happy home but now it's too late.

All I can see are the big green tanks,
As I watch with my daughter from the top of the bank.

Tears from my daughter drop onto my hand,
I shiver with fear as I look at the land.

The snow-covered mountains surround me by night,
All I can feel are my fists tight with spite.

I feel lonely and cold, I'm away from my wife,
Is this a dream or just a terrible life?

Hypnotised by the still of the day,
I can't go on, I walk away.

Hannah Burrows (13)
Hele's School

My Mum

My mum is busy, she never stops,
She looks after the family, washes and cooks.
I tell her all my problems and she makes them go away,
I love her and with her I want to stay.
Mum has brown hair which is permed,
She is a special friend.
We're very close, at least that's how I feel.
She works hard at home and at work,
Yet she still has time for me.
She is always on her feet and never rests,
Myself I think she is the best.

Celtie Fuller (11)
Hele's School

RACING CARS

One o'clock strikes
Anyone for a fag?
The engines start to run
There goes the flag!

With a rising cheer
And a manager's scream
And a radio hum
And an engine's brum.

Squeaking of wheels
A smash and a crash
A hum and a whistle
And gales being bashed.

Technicians screaming out
Crowds beaming
Wheels squealing out
Managers shouting out.

Big flags swinging
People crying
Racers happy, racers sad
People smiling.

Engines blow up
Anyone for beers?
A hurricane of cheers
An eyeful of tears.

Quieting of crowds
In come the rain clouds
Quieting of crowds and cars
All gone to the bars!

Paul McDonnell (13)
Hele's School

MY POEM ABOUT CRICKET

I put on my kit, the Ashes had arrived.
As I walked out of the tunnel and onto the pitch,
I saw all those eyes from above
And I thought cricket, what a game.

With my bat in one hand, ball in the other,
I take my place on the field.
The atmosphere is fab.
Then the game begins.

I bowl first . . . as I run I think I'm flying.
Then the ball leaves my hand, oh what a bowl.
It bounces towards the wickets,
And then there is silence.

The ball hits the wickets,
The batsman is out.
That was my moment of glory,
And I enjoyed it.

Mark Lewis (13)
Hele's School

CHINESE

As I look at thin baby, sweet and kind,
Underneath lies a terrible mind.
What will she turn out like, when she's older,
Will it be mean or will it get colder?
Wrapped in a bundle,
As tight as can be.
The little tiny baby, quiet as can be.

Claire Hudson (13)
Hele's School

FROM MY WINDOW

Looking from my window
What do I see?
Big city buildings in
Front of me.

I wish the view was green,
Like a glossy magazine,
So much concrete I have seen,
I wish I lived somewhere clean.

I wish the sky was clear
To see the birds so near,
Instead of what I see here,
All the city smog!

I wish I saw a deer,
Running in the clear,
What I see here,
Is nowhere near!

Stacey McKenzie (13)
Hele's School

WHAT'S OUT THERE?

What's out there?
Beyond the stars,
An alien race
Or just dark space?

What's out there?
Beyond the stars?
The things we see,
What can they be?
Just some clouds,
Or shooting stars?

What's out there?
Beyond the stars.
Things of amazement,
Or nothing at all.
The more we wonder,
The more we seem to see.
I want to know what's out there,
It all amazes me.

Christopher Golden (13)
Hele's School

THE RICH GIRL

The rain pours down as she steps out the door
She's the girl who's got everything but wants so much more
The tears on her cheeks roll down her face
She remembers the times, she's so out of place.

She clenches her fists as she walks down the path
Maybe she's free, maybe at last
The fists are of fear, anger and pain,
Life as she knows it, won't be the same.

She thinks to herself as she runs out the gate
This might be her biggest mistake
Daddy says running away is for cowards
If only he knew, could see through the showers.

So now she's walking away from the gate
Away from the anger, away from the hate,
She can make it on her own, she's sure
'Cos she's the girl who's got everything, but wants so much more.

Vicki Osmond (13)
Hele's School

ELEPHANT

I was an elephant
As happy as can be
Along came a hunter
Who shot me.

Now my feet are bins
And my tusks sit on a table
If you were an elephant
Your life would be unstable.

Poachers were here
Poachers were there
They have killed me
And they just don't care.

Gavin Shelton (13)
Hele's School

THE PIER

The pier stands long, tall and strong,
It stands in the sea
Ready to entertain you and me.

The people line up for hours on end
To get into the theatre
To watch the play again and again.

But when it gets late
And the people have gone home
The pier stands, all alone.

Mark Lunn (14)
Hele's School

TOM PIKE

Tom Pike walked into the corner shop,
With hair like twigs on a tree,
With eyes like shells and a beak for a nose,
An old baggy T-shirt,
And trousers with holes.

He had enough to buy something for £1.00.
That would do for gin.
People looked, people stared,
And walked right past with a grin.

Tom Pike never knew his mother,
She died when he was five.
He went to school in what he wore,
But never learnt a thing,
So now he lives alone.

He has no home to live in,
As he walks through the street.
An unknown path he leads,
Down a winding street of mystery.

But at the end of the day,
He says a prayer for people poorer than him,
And thanks God for his life.
Amen, Amen.

Maria Whyatt (13)
Hele's School

HYPNOTISED

As I look into space
I see the dark sky,
Everything so quiet
As the train rolls by.

Am I death
Or am I blind,
Or have I been hypnotised
By the space of time?

Every hour, every day
The unknown secrets
By the power
Of the day.

I feel sleepy
But yet amused,
Am I guarding the station
Or waiting for news?

Bombs and bangs
Black and blue
What's going on?
I haven't a clue.

Leanne Stephens (13)
Hele's School

STATUE

Little statue standing there,
As quiet as can be.
I think people mock,
Because I'm made of rock.

Little statue standing there,
As quiet as can be.
I think people disguise me,
Because I'm ugly as can be.

Jonathon Evans (13)
Hele's School

MY HOPES FOR THE FUTURE

Everyone wishes for money,
or to marry the next film star,
but when you look at reality,
a wish just doesn't come true.

I want to be in the navy,
and that is a thing I can do,
I will sign up as an officer,
to follow in my father's steps.

I hope to make a family,
have two kids or more,
to be healthy and sporty,
and to be a friend to others.

There could be cures for diseases,
such as cancer and AIDS,
if scientists keep working,
others could live more days.

I want to stop pollution,
war and poverty,
I just wish there could be peace,
and happiness for you and me.

Sam Hughes (11)
Hele's School

FOOTBALL

Once again that time is here
When people shout and people cheer
Kicking, passing, scoring too
Stay there mate, I'll pass to you
Goalie in, goalie out
Yes, that's a goal, hear them shout
Linesman running right and left
Who's in black? That's the ref
Slide and tackle that's the way
It's real fun to watch them play
It's real warm, the weather's fine
The whistle goes, it's half-time
A piece of orange, a little chat
Come on lads let's get back
Running, sliding, slipping too
Get the ball and take it through
Penalties, free kicks, corners too
Look out goalie I'm coming through.

Simon Jones (13)
Hele's School

EXCITEMENT

Excitement is the scrappy waves of the sea,
Jumping, busy waves crashing
Stones jumping out of the sea.
The sea is excited!

Excitement is a dog,
Alert, chasing every noise heard
Jumping, running, he will never stop.
The dog is excited!

Excitement is thunder and lightning,
Flashing, roaring and flying
Beaming through the air.
The thunder and lightning is excited!

Excitement is loud heavy metal music,
Banging a base drum
Your heart's beating fast.
The music is excited!

Jason Jones (12)
Hele's School

Penguins' Slide

Fun are the days on our slides
From top to bottom and around again
Up and up to the top we waddle
Then back down, don't stop in the middle.

Bart on first, bravest of all
Then it's Millhouse waiting to go
While William at the top 'Oh no I can't go down.'

Days of joy, the sun is out
Us three out having fun
We hear Mum shout
'Come on you three it's time for tea.'
'No,' we shout with our faces in a glee
At the end of the slide the water is bright.

Up and down we go until it's night
Next day here along with the sun
Great we all think it's time for more fun.

Chloe Jenkins (12)
Hele's School

THE SHARK

He clasps his prey,
With vicious jaws.
Close to the surface,
His fin appears.

He swims around,
Making no sound.

And when the seals,
Come out to play.
The shark begins to
Hunt for prey.

We humans have learnt
To fear the shark.
But I see no reason
To put them in the dark.

Hayley Salvage (13)
Hele's School

THE LOST RACE

Is it a cross,
Can it fly,
Is it a woman or a butterfly?
This mythical beast is deranged,
Are its abilities very ranged?

This freak of beauty
It is so bizarre,
Where did it come from,
How far, how far?

Michael Kinver (12)
Hele's School

FASHION

Tesco's, Tesco's where you buy your best clothes,
Two pound fifty, cheap and nifty,
Knee length skirts and knee high socks,
So last Tuesday now it's frocks,
Top Shop, Miss Selfridge, and Kookai,
Give me some of that any day.
So don't forget,
Tesco's, Tesco's, where you buy your best clothes,
Two pound fifty, cheap and nifty.
If you do, no doubt about it,
You'll be this year's main fashion crisis.
So pull down those socks and roll up those skirts,
And you'll be the coolest kid there is.

Hannah Conman (12)
Hele's School

THE MOTHER AND ITS FOAL

One Saturday afternoon we went up to see the foal,
She stood near her mother obviously feeling anxious,
Its wobbly legs and knobbly knees made her a bit unstable.
The mother came trotting up thinking we had some food for her.
The foal came trotting after her, wobbling along.

Later on in the evening when we came back,
The mother and her foal stood against a high hedge,
And the sleepy, tired foal lay down and went to sleep,
And a little while later the mother joined her.

Samantha Ferrand (12)
Hele's School

PARADISE

In a boat far away
a boy looks at the palm trees sway.
He sees such a beautiful beach
he stretches out, it's out of reach.

The sea is clear as day
the beach is still far away.
In front of you your paradise looms
where plants and trees are in bloom.

There's a tiny splash
as the waves crash.
The sand is getting hot
he's already picked his spot.

The sand is like grain
looks like no rain.
He looks at his paradise beach
it's still out of reach.

As he turns it fades away
he sees the palm trees sway.
Then he sees this empty beach
that is still out of reach.

Carly Luffman (12)
Hele's School

KALEIDOSCOPE

The kaleidoscope makes me feel dizzy,
it goes round and round with a very whisk noise,
its bits of glass go round and round with
all the bright colours and it makes me feel so good.

The kaleidoscope is so colourful and looks all very attractive,
its spinning glass and whizzing colours are all too much for me,
the kaleidoscope is so colourful and makes me wonder why?

Lois Oliveira (11)
Hele's School

LONELINESS

Loneliness is autumn:
You are a leaf falling further and further
   Away towards nothingness.
Loneliness is a foggy day:
You are surrounded by nothing
   No one in sight.
Loneliness is black
Sad and dull
   Alone and isolated.
Loneliness is a calm sea -
No surfers, no swimmers
   No boats.
Loneliness is an isolated countryside
As you stand alone
   Next to a bare tree.
Loneliness is a piano solo,
   Slow and tedious.
Loneliness is cold
Frost and ice
   On a dark day.
Loneliness is a snail
Trundling along
   Alone in the world.

Jennifer Joinson (12)
Hele's School

THE ROWERTEERS

As they fly through the water so fast,
The water gushes right past,
A bridge comes nearer,
And under that go they,
So fast as if they want to catch a prey.
And so they do, the finish line,
But still a long way to go till they can be fellows of fine.

Their bones ache, their muscles tense,
As they draw nearer to the finish line.
They know what waits them,
A trophy of pine, but it's a long way to the finishing line.
The finishing line is now in sight,
And it gives them a fright.
The team battle on twice as hard,
And the final metres of the call of 'Row'.

At last they are fellows of fine
And of course, not to forget they get the trophy of pine.

Simon Bevans (12)
Hele's School

WHALE POEM

As swift as the ocean waves
The great whale comes up to bathe
Her eyes hold secrets warm not cold
None of them are ever told.
Gently and beautiful as she may be
Hunters still kill her kind for happiness and glee
She moves slow with her calf at her side
Protecting him from dangers above, she hides.

The calf clings on his mother's back
Dozing, not knowing his life is packed
A roaring sound enters the whale's ears
Alerts the mother she feels her calf's fears.
The hunter's vessel appears on the water
A spear shots ready to slaughter
The mother whale is hit, she falls slowly
Her calf cries, his heart becomes lonely.

Rebecca Radmore (12)
Hele's School

THE TIGER

The tiger lays upon the ground,
Gazelles are jumping round and round.
His fearful eye rests on the deer,
A thumping sound that a world could hear.
His heart starts pumping, his
Claws shoot out,
Then one gazelle made a
Mighty shout.
The tiger jumped a giant jump,
And came back down with a
Thunderous thump.
The tiger clawed in, pulled a
Gazelle down.
It struggled and reached to
Get off the ground.
He chewed all the flesh
While the others ran on,
By the time he had finished,
The rest, they had gone.

Daniel Ford (12)
Hele's School

APPLE PIE

Yummy, yummy, scrumptious, nice
With added vitamins and a sprinkle of spice
Tasty apples at their best
Ready to go into my stomach and digest.

I like to eat my apple pie hot
Red hot, steaming in a pot
It goes on for minutes
It bubbles out apple bits.

As it comes out piping hot
I like my pie, in fact, quite a lot
I eat it with a tablespoon
I like it after lunch at noon.

I want to say there is enough
The problem is no chocolate stuff
I look in the cupboard and see
A chocolate bottle in front of me.

I see it in the corner of my eye
I cannot wait to get stuck into that pie
I dig in with some force
With sugar and a syrupy sauce.

Two minutes, it is all gone
I saw it, it really shone
Have no money for another one
I might as well do with a sticky bun.

Steven Peck (12)
Hele's School

IN MY FAMILY

In my family,
There's people young and people small,
There's people old and people tall.

First there's my mum, second my dad,
Third my brother, he is really bad,
Fourth there's my gerbil, he is really cute,
Fifth there's my sister who deafens me on her flute,
And last of all, the best to see,
He's courageous and handsome,
Yes it's me.

Seventh it's my grandad, who tells me about the war,
Eighth there's my nan who's a spritely ninety-four,
Their grandson is great to see,
He's courageous and handsome,
Yes, it's me.

Ninth there's my Uncle Sam,
Who's married to Auntie Jane,
And last of all my cousins,
Who live just down the lane.

I'd love to go on further,
And tell you about the rest,
But by now I'm sure you know,
I'll always be the best.

Thomas Quirke (12)
Hele's School

THE CAT

I have a cat called Jackson
He likes to sneak around
But when he hears a loud noise
He jumps 3ft off the ground.

Then when he is hungry
He jumps up on the side
And when his food is on his tray
He sniffs it and goes outside.

My cat Jackson can be a big pain
When we put on his flea collar
He takes it off again.

He can be rather vicious
But also very calm
He can be very playful
But he can do a lot of harm.

The reason his name is Jackson
Is because he's black and white
And Michael Jackson sings this
And they both are very bright.

My poem is going to end now
You've learnt about my cat
I hope that you've enjoyed it
And ask me to come back.

Calum Baker (12)
Hele's School

My Goldfish

I've a goldfish, slippery and wet
Gold all over, and not a bad pet
As long as you don't expect too much
They're not like a rabbit in a hutch.

They spend their time in a tank
With pebbles and ferns and a boat with a plank
In and out of a cave they swim
I love to watch their feathery fins.

There they are just swimming
Without a care in the world
They come to the top to get some food
Because they have nothing else to do.

Their lives must be so empty
All on their own
Swimming through the plant life
And passing the diver and stones.

Maybe the reason for their boring lives
Is their short three second mind?
Swimming back and forth they go
Right up high and down quite low.

Off they swim into their den
To start the cycle all over again.

Darryl Webb (12)
Hele's School

COKE!

Bottles and cans,
Of fizzy Coke.
They made Santa,
That jolly red bloke,
He featured on telly,
With his jelly-like belly,
That famous company called Coke.

Brown liquid fizzing here and there,
They have a mascot polar bear,
It tastes quite sweet,
It's a nice treat,
For adults and kids galore.

Coke, Coke, that wonderful stuff,
If you don't like it, then that's tough,
It's the world's most popular drink,
Hundreds of cans are sold as you blink,
The cans of Coke are always red,
They couldn't be changed to pink instead.

Tasty soda,
The gorgeous odour,
That could only describe C*oke!*

Fizz, fizz, bubble, bubble,
Buying Coke is no trouble,
It takes up loads and loads of shelves,
Not even room for tiny elves.

Adam Leaves (13)
Hele's School

WORLD WAR II

Sirens screaming
Screaming people
People panicky and petrified
Petrified of bombs
Bombs drop from planes
Planes bring devastation
Devastation across the world
World demolished
Demolished by Germans
Germans bombing
Bombing houses
Houses destroyed
Destroyed by bombs
Bombs destroy everything
Everything gone.

Jamie Hembrow (11)
Hele's School

BEING ME

Being me is like being a book half written,
Not knowing what will happen next.
Like a ship bobbing up and down,
Good days, bad days, good day, bad day.
It's like a big hill you have to climb
But not knowing what's on top.
It's like a problem which you have to solve,
But it never seems to end.
It's like being unable to wake up
From a dream, or nightmare.

Ashleigh Mitchell (12)
Hele's School

PICTURES IN THE SKY

A cloud, a friend
Makes funny pictures
Like an elephant or a roaring dragon
As I gaze up to the clouds
It's like a lonely world
So peaceful and blind.

I hate when clouds get angry
Hailstones attack my kind eyes
Umbrella, umbrella please help
The stones attack me
If they touch they sting
Ouch! Please let the sun out.

Victoria Chudley (12)
Hele's School

MY POEM

A hamster, a hamster is a rock.
Sad and not much excitement
just a small sad thing that
moves and eats and has
lots of fears because it is
small and other things are bigger
than it, as thick as fog, as sad as me.

The mountains, mountains are
skyscrapers, really high and cold,
big things that don't have a life
just tall pieces of rock.
As high as the sky, as sad as me.

Fog, fog is a confusing thing
that hovers everywhere and
confuses you because you can't
see through it. It's just as thick as a cloud,
high up in the sky, as sad as me.

Dominic Forsyth (12)
Hele's School

EXCITEMENT

Excitement is a ball
Bouncing up and down.
A kitten playing, chasing, pouncing
Waiting for its dinner bowl.
Hail pounding down out of the sky
Surprising but cheering up the people below.
It is spring.
Full of hope, plants springing up from the ground
Slightly warming the cool world.
The choppy sea.
Waves crashing onto the rocks again and again.
Waves so high they flood the tiny beach.
Excitement is a thermometer showing temperatures rising
Quicker and quicker.
Excitement is yellow
Bright, unexpected, happy.
Rock 'n' roll music
So good that you don't want it to end.
When it does
Those warm, fuzzy feelings
Are hard to shake away.

Lindsey Denford
Hele's School

ANGER

Anger is a tiger
Trying to get some food.
He is orange and brown.

Anger is a river
Running fast and heavy.
It is rough and loud.

Anger is lightning and thunder
Loud and bright on a summer's day.
It is hot and bright. The tiger is angry and is very hot.

He is like the sea
Smashing against the rocks.
The water is deep blue like on a cold winter's day.

He erupts like a volcano with heavy, loud and hot lava.
It is loud and rough and it is very angry.
It smashes up the houses and rips up the trees.

Rebecca Hensman (12)
Hele's School

STRESS

S tress is a stormy day
T he sky is black
R ain is battering the roof top
E verywhere is full of puddles
S inging a tune, the wind whistles through a vent
S wooping leaves wet with the rain smash against the window.

Philip Partridge (12)
Hele's School

BATTLE POEM

The clang and clatter as the soldiers
and their weapons marched into battle.
The field was damp and muddy
it was midnight and the
heartless enemy strode up front.
The soldiers went to meet their doom
in the mud and blood mixed field
but they had a reason, they were fighting
for their king and country.
The battle had started.
The wails and cries of
injured and dying soldiers
sounded all over the battlefield.
At last the king from the other side
fell and ours still stood,
but too many lives had been lost.

Alice Evans (12)
Hele's School

INSIDE ME

Inside me,
I don't know why,
But I've always thought there's a little fly,
Working around, wherever may be,
Always doing jobs, whatever could they be,
Pumping the blood, working the brain,
Maybe he's just totally insane.

Hannah Saunders (11)
Hele's School

SADNESS

Sadness is a drizzly day,
Making the ground muddy and slushy.

Sadness is Eeyore the donkey,
Winnie the Pooh's friend who's always sad.

Sadness is autumn,
When everything is dying.

Sadness is the sea,
When it is rough, so rough, too dangerous to swim.

Sadness is loads of mountains,
So many you'll get lost.

Sadness is cold,
So cold it's ice.

Sadness is black,
So black you can't see anything.

Sadness is sad music,
So sad and quiet you can hardly hear it.

Sadness is slow,
Just like a snail.

Sadness is tears,
Tears running down your cheeks.

Emma Finnimore (12)
Hele's School

JOY IS...

Joy is a squirrel.
Free as a bird,
Happy as the summer,
Playfulness is the squirrel.

Joy is the sun.
Warm as yellow,
Bright is the sun,
Warmth is my joy.

Joy is fun.
Happiness is games,
Life is fun,
Joy is life.

Joy is life.
Trees as tall as mountains,
Waterfalls forever falling,
Life is in the lake.

Joy is friends.
Friendship is my mates,
Happiness is life,
Joy is *you!*

Peter Travers (12)
Hele's School

LOVE

Love is a butterfly, it makes you
flutter about with joy.

Love is a fresh, sunny day.
Hot weather and pure blue sky.

The sea is nice and calm,
smooth, it has no waves,
no ripples, it looks warm.

I feel like I am on a deserted island
with palm trees and a beach.
The sand is hot, sometimes it is boiling.

The colours that I think of are
fluorescent purples, oranges,
yellows and greens.

I like to listen to music about love
when I am in love like -
Teaspoon, Celine Dion,
Toni Braxton and Mariah Carey.

Kimberley Brooks (13)
Hele's School

YOU

You're the kind of person,
who makes me very proud,
you're someone who's so wonderful,
you stand out from the crowd.

That's why I'm warmly hoping,
today will truly be
as very happy for me
as you make life for me.

I look into your photo's eyes,
your face smiles back at me,
how I wish you'd realise,
how happy we could be.

Sadie Harden (11)
Hele's School

School Dinners

School dinners may seem very nice,
but most of it is made from lice.
Chips, chips are eaten a lot,
but the sauce it comes with is made from snot!

A ripened fruit will make you squirm,
since inside crawls a worm.
All that food becomes a handful,
but there's a slug between each mouthful.

Gone-off mash is slopped on your plate,
beware, beware this is your fate.
Now comes the insect pie,
now is the time for you to die!

Vegetables made from rats and nuts,
if you eat it you've got guts.
Don't eat that you nerds,
or you'll be saying your last words.

You have a choice of dry black mustard,
or mouldy, cold and lumpy custard.
Snail flan has lots of layers,
it's time for you to say your prayers!

Michael Bennett (12)
Hele's School

Happiness Poem

Today is a happy day, I can feel it in the air.
Today is a bouncy day, like a squirrel bounding in a tree.
Today is a warm day, when you get that feeling
inside your tummy when you laugh.
Today is an exciting day, with butterflies and bees,
flying and fluttering past a field of green, fresh, lush grass,
with buttercups and daisies with middles as bright as
the centre of the sun, while a calm, cool lake of
ice-cold water flows past.
A robin perched on the end of a branch starts to sing
a beautiful song of summer. In a nearby cottage, a familiar song
plays . . . that's it, flight of the bumblebee.
Today is a loud day, like a hyena laughing out loud.
Today is a calm day, when the sea is so calm it looks like
a gigantic pond, just sat there so peaceful and quiet
until the laughter starts again.

Teresa Hamley (12)
Hele's School

My Family

I live with my mum, my dad and my brother,
We all live together with one other.

Which is my sister who's three years old,
She's got lots of hair and my dad is bald.

My brother's a pest and also a pain,
When he's around he drives me insane.

Most of the days we all get on fine,
I like having this family that I can call mine.

Steven Peters (11)
Hele's School

SAMMY

This is Slimy Sam,
He is my pet snail,
He's all sticky and gooey,
And makes my mum go pale.

I took him to school,
To my mates he was shown,
But I was a fool,
He's now flat on the road.

Now, I am sad,
The driver is bad,
He who decided to travel,
Over Sam who went splat,
On the gravel.

Matthew Anstey (11)
Hele's School

MY GRANDAD IS A BOXER

My grandad is a boxer,
He has fists like tree trunks,
His body's like a steamroller,
And he punches better than most,
He kills like a tiger,
Looks like a rhino,
Beat up Prince Naseem,
Ripped off Tyson's head,
Then he met the Queen,
Now he's somewhere else,
Somewhere in a corner,
Down the pub with half a lager.

Andrew Barr (11)
Hele's School

HURRICANE!

There's a soaring monster in the sky
Blowing, roaring. I wonder why?
With an angered look on his fierce face,
He glides along at a light speed pace.

He weaves in and out of the trees,
Blowing all the autumn leaves,
Why has he come to ruin our lives?
Our lives of happiness, laughter - they're so nice!

He fills the air, he flies around,
With a blowing, roaring, whistling sound,
Down pours the rain, the tipping rain
Like a million tiny beasts on my window pane.

Gillian Hawke
Hele's School

WHERE HAVE THEY GONE

Which way did they go?
This way, that way?
Up or down

Did they catch the bus to town?
If you see them in the park
Tell them to come home
When it gets dark.

Michael Francis
Hele's School

THE WOODS

Creeping up on you like tigers searching for prey,
Umbers, crimsons and greens,
Wrap yourself around and capture the warmth,
Feel like a patchwork quilt.

Always darkness, never day
The beauty dulled by diamond black;
Whistle with the wind, swirl with the leaves,
Feel like an oval of umber.

The thousands of people, peering, glaring,
Colliding their leaves like a hurricane's swirl,
Deleting the world outside, beyond it,
Making magical worlds appear.

Lucy Ellis (11)
Hele's School

THE SUN

The sun rises,
Up and up,
People going down to the beach,
Trying to get burnt,
But the sun goes down and down,
People going home,
The sun goes to bed,
Silence in the night as the moon comes
Out to play.

Naomi Jones (12)
Hele's School

MY SISTER

This is my sister
on her foot is a blister
which she moans about all day.
She's got a job
with Uncle Bob
but her money he won't pay.

This is my sister,
nobody ever kissed her.
She's all lonely and sad.
I got her a horrid boyfriend
I think he's around the bend
but she doesn't think he's that bad.

Stephen Cole (11)
Hele's School

GORGON

When you catch her eye
It would be the last thing you
See; you won't run or cry
If you're brave you will seek her out.

You won't get far for you want a peek
You can't outwit her. You're too tempted
So tempted you're looking hard in the cave
Until! The rumours are true and! That's
It: You're cemented.

Luke Williams (11)
Hele's School

The Storm

I know the storm is getting annoyed
It's a sneaking, creeping cat
Roaring like a lion
He's sending rain and hail
As his tail against my window.

Now you know he's getting angry
He's throwing bolts of fire
He makes them flash
He makes them plunge
Into the deep beyond.

Now you know he's really mad
His lashing tail goes on
He's watching and roaring
As fire bolts plunge into the night.

Now you know he's in a rage
He sends a mighty bolt
His lashing tail kicks and swings
He lets out one almighty roar
That echoes through the night.

Now the storm is settling down
He stops his rain of fire
His lashing tail eases off
And the dark clouds float away.

Now all that's left of his mighty rage
Is running rivers in sodden streets.

Jodie Pay
Hele's School

THE WORLD THAT WAITS FOR NO ONE

I sat there gazing out of the steamed window
Watching the world rush by
and wondering if it will

Stop

and wait for me.
The car halts
and I step out into the world
and smell the air of a soft September

Morning

I pause for a moment and look up
at a tall, white building.
I feel like a small mouse
in a world that I neither understand or
communicate with,
I step inside the building

Slowly.

In this world I realise that time waits
for no one. Before me a bed with
my name on it. The old clock strikes 8.40

Time to go

Another bed is wheeled
To my bedside. I am tied
to it, and like a silver chariot it rolls
down the hallway, until it reaches
another tiny room with lots of

Gadgets and devices.

Slowly I'm injected and the world
starts to go dark. When I awake a blur is a
picture I am getting and I realise I'm
Back in the world that

Waits for no one.

Lisa Lubman (11)
Hele's School

STORM

Last night I heard a strange sound outside,
I pulled back the curtain and looked,
Flashing lights,
Trees blowing,
The crash of the monster's feet as he crept closer,
He rattled the windows with his mighty hands,
His cold breath swept through the house
Sending shivers down my spine.
Bang!
Flash!
His eyes were glinting,
His mouth was watering,
His hands were getting closer,
Trying to grab and drag me back with him
To his scary world,
And then, he died.

Katie Raven
Hele's School

IF I COULD HAVE ONE WISH

If I could have but one wish
It would be for you to become a fish
So you could swim through the sea
So you could come and see
Me!

Charlotte Procter (11)
Hele's School

SCARED OF THE SUN

It was at my gran's,
A hot summer's day,
I was scared,
Scared of the
reds, the yellows and oranges.
It was the sun.
Scared of the sun I was.
Scared like a mouse chased
by a cat.
Tried not to cry.
Just put my hat over my eyes.
I screamed.
I screamed until my mum
came out.
She took me in.
I was relieved,
It was like running out of air,
then finally getting it back again.
I've calmed down now,
Now that I'm in,
I'll go out again when the
Sun's gone in.

Adam Brimacombe (12)
Hele's School

KALEIDOSCOPE

A kaleidoscope has beautiful patterns,
Patterns like flowers,
Flowers filling the circles,
Circles made with faces,
Faces looking happy.

I can fall asleep thinking of the beautiful
Patterns on the kaleidoscope,
Kaleidoscope can be anything,
Anything just anything.

Carla Wilkinson (11)
Hele's School

IT SMASHED ON THE FLOOR

We walk outside to the top of the steps
Which spiralled, a long black snake.
Spiderman swung onto the arm rail.
He had only been bought yesterday,
The result of a long time saving.
My brother asked for a go and I said 'Yes.'
Now I ask myself why?
And then it fell.
One moment crawling along the high-rise building,
The next a parachutist who forgot his parachute.
And what happens to parachutists who forget their parachutes?
We rush down the black snake
To find his pieces violently separated.
Now I want to explode.
To say it was him, him, him,
But I'm a guest,
And decide to let him be scared.
My dad glues him back together.
Piecing his whole life back together
And part of mine.
My brother asks for a go and I say 'No.'

Nicholas Jones (12)
Hele's School

BIKE CRASH!

I could not ride a bike
Yet I was excited to ride on Dad's.
I sat on the crossbar
So high but loving it all the time.
My feet were nowhere near the ground
Balanced up there, I clenched on with all my might,
The birds singing and the trees rustling.
Yet one thing comforted me as we soared along the track.
It was my dad, he made me feel safe.
Then for some horrible reason, I had an urge
An urge I could not stop from swirling around in my head.
I did it, but soon regretted it.
The loveliness stopped, everything stopped.
The bike was on the ground, the wheel bent
Dad was on the floor,
He nearly went over the cliff.
I cried,
Cried with the agony I felt.
My leg was throbbing
All the skin had gone
Dad got up, picked me up.
I could not walk, not even hobble.
Dad tried to take the bike and me.
A lady came.
She took us to her car.
She drove us to the doctor's
They bandaged it up,
So we all went home.
That night I had nightmares about putting my foot
In the wheel of Dad's bike.

Carly Evens (12)
Hele's School

NEW LIFE

I was three,
Fresh air
Vibrant sun
Gentle breeze,
I walked
Under trees
Through woods.

Sun dimmed
Mysterious
Flicker through treetop canopy,
Like crackling fire
Tall, dark, looming,
Trees watch over me.

Whispering of birds
Scurry of squirrels,
A spectrum of colour
Brown, green, red,
Beams of light
Hit patches of bluebells
Like an underwater world.

On to hill top
Grass
Glistens with dew.
Odd white patches
Of daisies,
For the love of nature.

Carl Johnston (11)
Hele's School

IN THE SEA

As I neared the sea, I felt the wind in my hair
and the cold, wet sand at my feet.
I had goose-bumps all over me and all I could hear
was the chitter, chatter of my teeth.
When I stepped into the water, my feet froze.
The waves were so big and the sea so rough.
But I ventured further, enjoying the excitement and danger
but disliking the coldness.
Suddenly a big wave came and went right over me.
I was pushed to the ground.
I pulled myself up again, seaweed in my face.
I turned around and a big, angry wave was on top of me,
I got dragged with it.
I thought I was going to die.
I hit the ground, then blacked out
for a few seconds.
I opened my eyes,
thoughts flashed through my head of dying,
then surviving.
I crawled up the beach
out of the sea,
determined not to go back in,
and give the huge, towering waves
a chance to take me again.

Lisa Elliott (13)
Hele's School

A Band Contest

One summer day our band gathered together
on a trip to the band contest.
It was a one hour bus trip.
There was extreme panic and noise.
We arrived at a huge high school.
The school was gigantic with endless hallways
and billions of different representatives
walking all around from all over Illinois.
The inside had the smell of band oil with bands going into rooms.
We were guided into a room and waited four hours for our turn.
People were nervous like a bride and groom on a wedding day.
After an hour, it seemed like a decade, two a century,
then lunch time and four a millennium.
Finally it was our turn.
We were taken to a monstrous room with a massive audience.
Our band played King Arthur's Processional.
Five judges were staring at us like vultures.
The judges were nicely dressed except one,
who looked like a Caribbean Santa.
We played, then it was my turn to do my solo.
The audience was glaring, quiet, yet excited.
I played. The audience cheered and a friend yelled,
'Congratulations, you are good.'
Another yelled 'So gifted.'
Havana scored 3rd of Illinois.
Everyone was relieved to speak on our bus trip home.
I still remember that day.

Erik T Brockwell (12)
Hele's School

A DAY EARLY

I woke up early feeling excited and scared
It was my first day at school today
My uniform hung all crisp and new on my wardrobe door
I packed my small bag with crisps and lunch
And started on my way.

Walking in the big playground with my mum holding my hand
Wondering why it was so calm and feeling very cold.
My shirt was stiff, my tie felt tight,
My shoes rubbed when I walked.
Climbing the steps 1, 2, 3,
Opening the door, the class was empty.
The chairs were empty, the tables were bare,
No children were sitting there.
Nervous! Worried! My mum started to *flap!*

Then I saw a lady coming to the door, Mum said
'That's your teacher.' I gave a big smile
She said 'What are you doing here?'
My face dropped.
My mum started to talk to her then I heard a voice
Whisper 'You're a day early.'
I got very sad. That's why there wasn't any children here.
I started to cry.
Mum said 'I am sorry' and gave me a smile.
'At least you know what to do
Tomorrow' she said.
I smiled.

Lindsay Boston (12)
Hele's School

KALEIDOSCOPE

September's gone, October's here,
Now the autumn's come,
Red, yellow, orange and green,
Leaves falling to the ground.
Twisting round and round,
Where they land we can only guess.
The colours all mixing together as if they're
Trying to be one united colour.
But when they're on the ground,
They are no longer together,
People trample on top of them,
Squash them and take them home on the bottom of their shoes.
Never to be seen again except on the doormat
Which is where they stay until they are shaken off,
No more fall but more grow in the spring
And the same thing happens all over again.

Suzanne John (11)
Hele's School

FAMILY

My dad, like the ships he travels on,
is away from home a lot.
Several times his face I forgot,
but never his wiry beard
or his jolly voice, I on the phone
have heard.
He is 6 feet high and very strong,
he inspects all new ships and is never wrong.
He's playful, friendly, funny and fair.
all around him is a wonderful air.

Owen Curtin (11)
Hele's School

MY HOPES FOR THE FUTURE

When I'm older I want
to live in the city
or by the sea
I also want to go to University.

Me and my mates want
to live together
in an apartment in
the city, and open a
clothes shop there.

But when I'm even older
and want to settle down
I'll want to buy a house
in the city with my
husband and have two kids.

I also want to enjoy
my life and live
in good health. I also want to
have loads of pets.

When I'm older I hope
the world will be
a much happier place
for you and me.

No more fighting
no more wars
we will live in peace.

No one will starve
or live on streets
and die so young.

The environment will
be cleaner and the
animals will live longer.
There will be no pollution
or fumes in the air.

We will make the world
a better place
you'll see
and make people care.

Becky Fairclough (11)
Hele's School

BROTHERS!

The trouble with my brother
although he's number one,
he's always ready to disrupt
he never thinks to stop his fuss.

Although I love him still,
he's a most annoying little pest,
who takes his chance to embarrass me
when he's trying to impress.

The trouble with my brother
is that he's an innocent looking pest,
so it's always me who gets the blame,
he ends up being best.

The best thing about my brother
although he is a pest,
is that he's always there for me,
so that is why he's the best.

Jo Williams (11)
Hele's School

MUM

My mum runs about the house
making sure it's clean.
Because she's very busy,
she never can be seen.

People say I look like her,
don't know if that's true.
Her favourite programme is,
NYPD Blue.

She sometimes takes me places,
where I need to be.
Sometimes hockey matches,
she's like a taxi.

I wish I could thank her
for everything she's done.
The main thing is -
that she is my mum.

Heather Carter (11)
Hele's School

MY COUSIN

My cousin makes me laugh
My cousin makes me happy
He plays cricket with me and teaches me
How to catch a ball when it is really high.
My cousin comes to stay at my house
Shares my room and complains about my snoring.

Christopher Higman (12)
Hele's School

LOVELY SHAPES

The kaleidoscope makes me feel ill
because it is really dizzy.
It has lots of different colours so that
it makes it nice and colourful.
It is in a small tub just so you
can fit your eye in the hole.

The kaleidoscope has lots of different colours
And things to see in it.
It makes me feel sleepy because
it is nice and relaxing to see and watch.

Sheree McIntosh (11)
Hele's School

MY GRANDAD

My grandad is fun and that is true.
He tells some good stories about the time he lived at Looe.
He always wears a funny hat,
And I certainly won't forget that.
He buys me presents when it's not my birthday,
And I won't forget the way,
That he laughs and tells jokes, they really are quite funny.
And when I go on holiday he gives me pocket money!

I really love my grandad, I don't know where I'd be without him.

Amy Giles (11)
Hele's School

PONIES

Dartmoor ponies, strong and bold
Standing in the winter cold.
On the moor in all kinds of weather
Standing alone or standing together.

Brave little ponies roaming free
There for all of us to see.
Brown and black ones, some are white,
Grazing happily into the night.

Hear their hooves pound as they run,
From laughing children having fun.
Hear them snort and hear them neigh,
As they stand there day by day.

Strong little ponies, no shelter there
From winter winds or the sun's hot glare.
Their home, a beautiful, magical place,
Where they can enjoy the open space.

Laura Harrington (12)
Hele's School

MY GRANDAD

My grandad's very special
I love him very much.
I'd never be without him or very far apart.
He has thin grey hair and pale blue eyes,
And although he says he hasn't, he has false teeth.
Every time the phone rings he waves his feet in the air
And does ten star jumps on the settee. Nan tells him off.
But guess what? He does it again!
He's the best grandad ever, I'd never swap him for the world.

Carly Thorpe (11)
Hele's School

My Kitten

My kitten 'Oscar' is jet-black and white.
He likes to go out when it's dark to fight.
Our other moggy, Bob, is black and fat,
He must be the most blackest, fattest cat,
Oscar is not fat, he's the normal size.
He has some very suspicious, strange eyes,
When it's feeding time they both have cat food,
After their meal they are in a good mood,
They like to play with hair bobbles and string,
At Christmas we always buy them something.
Oscar likes playing with our big rabbit,
But he always tries to bite and grab it.
They both like playing with the cat next door,
But it always ends with a great big war!

Sophie Taylor (11)
Hele's School

My Dad

My dad is very nice,
But sometimes he will shout
And he's got the funniest jokes about.

He makes me do my homework,
Or my TV is taken away,
If I still don't do it
I'm not allowed out to play.

But then I suppose, if he didn't,
My homework,
Would never be done.

Timothy Hext (11)
Hele's School

SEASONS

Winter brings you frost
And snow,
Children wrap up warm from
Jack Frost and cold.

Next comes spring,
Where the birds like to sing
And flowers appear,
Soon summer will be here.

Summer brings
The hot sun,
Where children like to go to the beach,
But soon it's all over.

Autumn brings the golden leaves
And trees will soon be bare,
It also brings the dark nights,
Winter will soon be here.

Rebecca Long (12)
Hele's School

CHRISTMAS

Christmas is happy for most,
but not for me.
Everyone gets presents,
but not me.
Joy is in the air,
but not in the air that I breathe.
Please God make me happy.

Christmas is a time for sharing
I have no one to share it with.
Christmas is warm and memorable
but I am cold and have nothing to remember,
Christmas is the same as the next day to me.
Please God make me happy.

Louise Rea (12)
Ivybridge Community College

SEALIFE

It swishes,
it swirls,
it glistens
in the sunlight.
Yes, the sea.
Where fish swim and creatures live.
Boats sail on it every day
making patterns as they go on their way.
Waves curling and pushing their way to the shore
it's a beautiful world down there.

Weed swaying in the currents,
and creatures being swept backwards,
by the incoming tide.
The gold, glistening sand
lying flat like a smooth, velvet curtain.
The unmistakable sound of the world beneath
showing off its beauty.

Jenny Purt (11)
Ivybridge Community College

THE EAGLE

The eagle is the pilot of a turbo
Super jet plane.
It survives in any weather, the
Wind, the sun, the snow and rain.

Its talons are as sharp as knives
And its eyes as bright as flames.
It frolics in the mountain air
Like a child at its games.

It's like a speeding bullet when
It swoops down on its prey.
But it really is a timid bird
In its own and private way.

Chris Pearson (12)
Ivybridge Community College

MY DESK

I open my desk,
and I am taken into
a world of happiness and fun.
I can run and run,
through the green grassy fields
I can laugh and play.
I shut my desk and
I whirl and whirl,
around I go,
and I land back at home
in my normal world.

Louella Benn (12)
Ivybridge Community College

AN ENVIRONMENTAL POEM

Look at the world now,
What have we done?
Tonight the moon, today the sun.
There are now lots of dead trees,
And also plants.
Dead wildlife everywhere, from elephants to ants.
Rainforests gone, trees have been knocked down,
Lots of dead humans, what an upsetting sound.
Killer whales in the sea,
Nature's love and world beauty.
Natural love from you to me,
Lots of chainsaws and also cranes,
Global warming causing flood-making rains.
Thunder storms and also droughts,
No one looks after the earth, that's what it's all about.
Earthquakes damage our beautiful earth,
Countdown to death from our birth
Rubbish everywhere, also in the sea,
Rubbish in the streets as far as the eye can see.

Peter Wilkes (14)
John Kitto Community College

AEROPLANES

Up, up, into the sky
Moving slowly, climbing
Watch as crowds go by.
Noisily the engines roar
Wheels drop down to the floor
People wait by the door
To get their bags
And away they go.

Jade Kingdom (12)
Pathfield Special School

VEGETABLES

Vegetables come in all sizes
They taste good and are full of surprises.
Some are sweet, some are sour,
Some will ripen by the hour.

Kevin Lidstone-Brown (12)
Pathfield Special School

WAVE

The wave was rolling forth,
Like a boulder tumbling onwards.
His crest was foaming
Like a rabid dog.
Bubbles of poisonous looking froth,
Bursting in explosions of terror.
The wave had a powerful structure,
Yet a sleek,
Streamlined figure he bore.
His head being stretched outwards,
With a strain
Like a bridge of suspension.
Spray was flying from his brow,
Like the mane of a fleetingly,
Galloping horse.
His glory was that of a silver stag,
Entwined with beauty,
Constantly renewed.
Then sharp,
Jagged rocks,
Broke his darting path.
He died being broken apart.
His glorious reign of the seas was run.
His life had been shattered,
Upon the shores of the coast.

Kristian Thaller (13)
Plymouth Hospital School

HORSE

Silky fur racing along the big strong muscles
Circling, covering the whole of the field
The strong breeze running through the tail
Dashing through a gust of wind careless of the world around him
Clip and clop ringing to my ears
As strong as a machine
Has feelings so deep but can never show them
A wild animal protecting its ground.

Emma Ackrill (13)
St James' High School, Exeter

PUPPIES

This mammal is trying to say something 'Listen.'
Look what I see before me, a small puppy standing proud.
Soft and furry, almost feels like new.
Sorrow in their eyes, head down low, sniffing, searching for their food.
Stands by the door and tries to say goodbye before I go to school.
Woof! Woof! Goes my dog.
Someone's making a dog sound 'Listen' carefully.

Danielle Smith (13)
St James' High School, Exeter

POETIC TECHNIQUES

Slimy, slithery, long and small
Hides in amongst the big, tall lawn.
All alone in a great big field,
Waiting for prey to arrive.
Small, flexible, big, beady eyes
Lives on its own watching by.
Rustling, crackling, hissing.
Hissing as it says hello.
Crackling as it slithers through the dried up leaves
Like a lord of its surroundings.
He is a really devious thing.

Sarah Milden (13)
St James' High School, Exeter

FIRE

A big orange flame moving by the minute
The fire burns as you touch it
The fire clicks by time
A fire is like the sun, hot and bright
A lamp, brightly shining in the dark
The fire is angry and kills people
Blowing as it lives
A light bright on the ground dying, dying, puff away it goes.

Richard Drew (13)
St James' High School, Exeter

MY MONKEY POEM

A small, quite fat, brown little monkey,
Like a pussy climbing a tree
Grovelling for his banana
Oh aa ohaa, the noise that they make
Monkeys whining on and on
Banana looking after its territory.
Monkey mania maybe his game
Walking around like people in the park.

Vicky Marks (13)
St James' High School, Exeter

TIGER POEM

The tiger's roar echoing in its surroundings
The brightness of the tiger's colours come shining through
A towering figure of a person protecting its territory
Creaking in its footsteps
Like an angel in its presence
Cold and comfy, croaking in its roar
The layer of its skin brings out human features
Its fur feels so rugged.

Daniel Kelly (13)
St James' High School, Exeter

A CAR

Silver, sleek and stylish.
Smooth, sensitive steering, strong and comfortable.
As aerodynamic as an eagle swooping around every corner.
The exhausts tuned and ready to rumble.
A tiger closing down on the wounded prey.
A beast in a shell just waiting to be free.
Tyres screeching, rubber sizzling and the radio blaring.
Like a person sprinting down the road, where he went nobody knows.

Ryan Joint (13)
St James' High School, Exeter

A VET

It feels sad worrying and caring
Like a giant caring for midgets.
The huge vet stands with a white coat on looking on sympathetically
Like a giant standing over the poor, weak animal.
Like a hedgehog working slowly, concentrating
Worrying conversations, drills drilling, hearts beating, oxygen pumping
Walking and standing worrying about a pet
Working, wishing willing . . .

Graham Hannaford (13)
St James' High School, Exeter

THE TREE

The wind is swaying to and fro.
The leaves are falling to the ground.
The trunk is standing still surrounded by autumn leaves.
The wind is whistling through the windows.
The branches are waving, crackling and falling.
The wind is blustery like a breath of air.
It's like a long-lasting hurricane or a whirlpool that's never-ending.
It's fresh and draughty like a person that extends and keeps going.
Whispering through the houses touching tree to tree.
The endless, everlasting wind keeps blowing forever more.

Kirstie Chrichard (13)
St James' High School, Exeter

LOVE

One big heart waiting to go bang,
Big and warm and soft,
Boom, boom is what you hear,
Like a warm blazing fire,
A fire keeping my body warm,
Loving everybody, is so kind
Saying I love you,
And whispering warm words.

Natasha Edworthy (13)
St James' High School, Exeter

The Cliff

A face of rock alone looking ever onwards at the ocean of blue,
Waves reaching at the ancient cliff face.
Strong, solid, stone with sunshine shining down.
Cold, roughened and worn by time.
Cracking, breaking, crumbling.
Ever crippled and hurt by the emotionless onslaught of waves.
Like a bullied child battered and hurt.
The sea's a punchbag taking punch after punch, far longer than
time itself.

Matthew Bradley (13)
St James' High School, Exeter

Rabbits

Soft and furry, warm to touch.
Long ears twitch in the wind.
Creeping up to its food like a tiger stalking its prey.
Bang! It jumps in and stamps its foot.
Showing its emotions clearly.
Quiet unless in a temper.
Racing round a rabbit run.
Like a car winning its first race.

Lucie-Mayre Bowden (13)
St James' High School, Exeter

FIRE BURNING

Hot and raging, red and orange
Hot and fierce, burns you to ribbons.
Roaring and cracking, caving in.
Like an orange, with no skin.
Like a couple in a fright.
Whoosh, crack bang and whistle.
Hot, heavy, hard to handle.
Terrible, frightening leaves you weak at your knees.

Tasha Arnold (14)
St James' High School, Exeter

WIND

It sounds like the sea and rivers.
Swoosh, whoosh, rattle of the letterbox.
You can see the grass moving from side to side very fast.
The wind whistles through the trees.
You can see dark shadows moving through the curtain swinging side to side.
When the wind goes through your body
It feels like ice going through your body.

Sean Melvin (14)
St James' High School, Exeter

SNAKE

It side-winds through the leaves
Flickering its forked tongued to taste for food.
Carefully and quietly slithering along,
The scaly, thin snake scents prey.
So cleverly and slyly sneaks along
Until it's in sight of a mouse.
Quicker than the eye can blink
The creepy, wicked snake is eating its prey.
Not chewing it fast, swallowing it whole.
The poison of the snake is venom
Poisoning the little creature so it is not to get away
And when it's finished disposes of the bones,
And off to home for another day.

Joe Doyle (13)
South Molton Community College

THE DOG

Bouncing around the country tracks without a worry or care,
its back legs swiftly move from side to side,
and the dog carries on bouncing around.

Its jet black ears poke up by a mile
it hears the murmurous birds swooping in the sea blue sky.
The dog's wet dribble seeps out from its mouth and covers the
                              track as it passes by.

It sees a rabbit and chases it far
its piercing bark gets stuck in your head.
The rabbit has gone in to the far away distance and the dog comes
                              back with a great big log.

Lizzie Scott (13)
South Molton Community College

BLACKBERRY PICKING

Long summer days are over,
Autumn's in the air.
Leaves are turning brown,
Summer flowers are gone,
Harvest time is here.
It's blackberry time again.

Trekking through cornfields,
Walking through wet grass.
Holding cans, tins and pots,
Looking for purple glossy clots.
Keeping your eyes on the hedge,
It's blackberry time again.

Looking for a plate of eyes,
Looking for black blobs.
Red and green ones are hard as a knot.
The ripening flesh is sweet.
Autumn's blood is on my shirt,
It's blackberry time again.

Eat them as you walk along.
Make a pot of jam.
Put them in a crusty pie,
When winter days are here.
Open up the freezer, open up the pot
Guess What? It's blackberry time again.

Jodie Hackman (13)
South Molton Community College

PADDY

Man's best friend,
Cuddly bundle,
Long shaggy coat which mud clings to,
Long licking tongue,
Small slim body,
Paw prints everywhere.
His marble eyes look big and bold,
Gulps water, crushes food,
Bounds and jumps everywhere he goes,
Nose to the floor any time of the day,
He's tired and weary,
He collapses in a shaggy heap,
It's a dog's life!

Robert Seatherton (13)
South Molton Community College

AVALANCHE

An avalanche is a huge mass of ice and snow.
It surges downwards at great speed.
Great avalanches occur on peaks,
    and mountainsides.
Heavy   snowfall.
Steep rocky slopes.
Large boulders.
Melting snow,
Avalanche!

Leighton Williams (13)
South Molton Community College

THE BULLY

Why pick on me? Just because
I'm short.
Why pick on me? I'm quite good at
Sports.

You stand taller than me. Most
People do,
But others don't pick on me, so
Why should you?

You think you're clever, as do your
Gang.
My friends say to ignore you
That's not an easy task.

Why do you bully me?
Other people don't.
Is it you're jealous?
Or were you a victim?

Why pick on me?

Stacey Phillips (13)
South Molton Community College

THE WHITE DEATH

Everything's silent
Everything's still
Until the avalanche strikes
Ready to kill.

It crashes down the mountainside
Nothing stands in its way
You'd better watch out
Or it might catch you, unaware.

When it hits
People are buried alive
In the end it comes to a
Standstill.

People are packed, trapped,
Dead or alive.

Fraser Bawden (13)
South Molton Community College

BUZZARD

Sailing high, soaring low
Going for the kill
Scanning the ground it zooms down
In for the kill.

Killing mice, voles, rats and rabbits
Ripping them to shreds
And all this just for the tender
Flesh of an animal, but it needs it to survive.

This fearsome creature
Soft to the touch
Streamlined in the air
Its beak as sharp as a knife.

It's seen by day
In the sky
Living its life alone
Living all alone, above the fast moving world.

Nicholas Strong (13)
South Molton Community College

THE SNOW MONSTER

Silence,
Stillness,
Nothing living in sight.
Calm mountainside,
Snow, white as white.
Blankets,
Engulfs,
The fresh green grass
As it falls from the sky,
And settles fast.
A bang,
A call,
The slightest sound,
Then it'll awake,
And come crashing to the ground.
With a roar
And great vibration
It rolls down the hillside
With terrific speed.
And like a monster takes over the land.
Hundreds flee,
Thousands die
As it hits the helpless village
Which sits in the valley below,
And it leaves only roughage.
When it's done its job
Of destroying and wrecking,
It finally comes to rest.
And, once again, after quite some time,
The mountains are filled with silence.

Amy Hill (13)
South Molton Community College

AVALANCHE

The snow is falling.
The ice is on the move, a huge avalanche appeared.

Boulders pound the snow, hurl it down the slope.

Pieces of rock fall away.
Sticky crystals slide, steep, rocky.

Avalanche!

Sudden wind gusts can trigger, trigger an avalanche.

Total destruction.
Piles of snow.
Death toll is massive.

Steven Holland (12)
South Molton Community College

AVALANCHE

Avalanche
Slippery, fast and rolling,
Ready to knock over
Anything in its way.
Steep slopes, icy pits.
Strong winds with great speeds.
Big lumps of snow rolling this way
All fine for the people
Not in the way!

Josh Britton (13)
South Molton Community College

AVALANCHE

Smooth surface,
heavy snowfall,
sudden winds
begin to blow
snow seeps through
slippery layers
of steepness of the slope.

A sudden clap of thunder,
falling icicle or an animal
crossing the slope, send sticky snow
tumbling down at great speeds,
slightest conditions are strong
to see through with a snowstorm
hurtling, swirling around and around.

Wet snow slides down
from high peaks on the mountains,
on a slippery slope's surface,
boulders are more deadly
for a death toll.

Marc Baker (12)
South Molton Community College

AVALANCHE

An avalanche is set off by the slightest noise.
An avalanche is in the Himalayas where there is steep rocky slopes.
The avalanche surges down at great speed.
An avalanche is a huge mass of ice.
Sticky snow picks up loose, snow crystals.

Justin Taylor (12)
South Molton Community College

AVALANCHE

Avalanche, huge mass of snow
surges downwards at great speeds from
high peaks in the Himalayas and Alps.

Wet snow, dry snow, slab avalanche
more deadly than ever as they swirl
huge chunks of solid, sticky wet and
dry snow as it breaks away layer from layer.

As an avalanche tumbles downwards and
leaves sparkly snow crystals
on the cold surface of the mountain
eventually the boulder stops and waits

for another noise to send it swirling down.

Mark Warren (12)
South Molton Community College

AVALANCHE

Avalanche, huge ice and snow surges, downward at great speed
Boulders deadly swirl down the high peaks.
Wet snow, dry snow, a slab avalanche!
All are deadly in different ways.
A huge chunk of solid, sticky snow breaks away from a slope.
A layer of loose crystals lying beneath the surface.
A snowstorm comes, new layers of snow build and build, and then
Avalanche!
Then all is quiet, and the avalanche is dead.

Brendon Pow (12)
South Molton Community College

AVALANCHE

Downhill into deadly dry snow
Wet snow, death toll speed.
Weight heavy snowfall.
Weight deep piles falling.
Explosion, noise, clap, thunder.
Surface creates slippery slope.
Wet snow, dry snow, deadly sticky snow.
Surfaces layers high from downhill.
Greatest speed breaks dry deadly snow.
Hundreds of crystals speed downhill.
Slippery, steepness, weight.

Tara Pengelly (12)
South Molton Community College

AVALANCHE

Snow seeps down.
After the snowstorm, snow settles.
Anchors to the mountainside.
Huge mass of ice and snow,
Surges at great speed.
Melting snow forms large boulders.
Solid, sticky snow breaks from slopes.
The avalanche reaches great speeds.
Hurtling downhill.
To smooth surface of gentler grass slopes.

Katie Blackmore (12)
South Molton Community College

AVALANCHE

Snowstorm, heavy snowfall
snow settles,
on anchored, rocky slopes with large
boulders.
Snow seeps on
smooth surface, solid sticky snow.
Icicles or twigs.
Silence.
Sudden wind or sloping
animals crossing, suddenly
Avalanche!
Hug mass of ice,
Death toll.

Katie Allibone (13)
South Molton Community College

CAT AND MOUSE

Prowling and creeping looking for food.
It's not much fun when he's in that mood.
He pounces, bounces and catches mice.
Playing with them as if they were dice.
As the mouse bravely breaks free.
The cat is going to lose his tea.
The cat bolts after the scurrying mouse.
Who heads straight towards a nearby house.
The mouse then leaps down a very small hole.
The cat cannot follow as he's not a mole!
The mouse it seems did get away.
The cat can wait another day.

Tom Bowman
South Molton Community College

AVALANCHE

Explosion, huge wet snow
surges downwards at great
speed.

Boulders gripping to
mountainsides.

Snow breaking up, swirling
down rocky slopes.

Death toll under layers of deep
thick, smooth snow.

Deafening noise as it rolls
downwards.

Ground shudders as snow hits
mountainside.

Expanding as snow joins
on, getting bigger.

Matthew Tearall (12)
South Molton Community College

AVALANCHE

Snow which breaks away from the mountainside.
Snow falls with great speed.
Snow rolls downhill.
Slides along, close to the ground.
Heavy snowfall all around.
Snow underneath, the trigger an avalanche.
The smooth surface of gentler grass covered slopes with snow.

Sam Clinkard (12)
South Molton Community College

SINKING

A splash of water touches my foot.
So cool, so inviting, dare I go?
Have I time to float away,
Out into the sea of my mind?
Another taste of the water I know,
Dragging me in, enticing me.
Will I be missed or noticed?
Can I escape from one magic moment?
I let myself drift out, faraway,
Gradually sinking to the depths
Of my imagination.
The water deafens me as I fall.
Oblivious in my daydream,
I am drowning.

Rosie Venner (15)
South Molton Community College

AVALANCHE

Big masses of ice
Big boulders of snow as it rolls downhill
Wet snow, dry snow, sticky snow
Heavy snowfall
Gripping, melting snow
Slippery layers of snow
Big snow crystals
Steep, rocky slopes.
Big boulders coming down at great speed
Flying down like one million
Elephants!

Maureen Simmonds (14)
South Molton Community College

UNTITLED

I wish I was always tidy
everyone in my class is tidy.
I always get shouted at.
It's not fair.
Everyone in my class doesn't.

I'm always late for school
no one else is.
The teachers always shouts at me
because I'm never there for a test.

I never have the right equipment for maths
so I am always asking to borrow equipment
and then the teachers are shouting at me
for asking.

Every time I forget my home work
the teachers are always moaning at me,
but when the other children forget their homework
the teachers are always kind.
It's not fair,
It's just not fair.

Darrell Haywood (12)
South Molton Community College

AVALANCHE

An avalanche is huge and icy
The snow surges downwards
At great speed.

Wet snow forms into large boulders
And rolls downwards.
Dry snow is deadly.
It swirls through the air.

A huge chunk of solid, sticky snow
Breaks away from a slope.
Loose snow crystals lying beneath the surface.

A slab avalanche hurtles itself down a slope
As new layers of snow settle onto the ground.
It binds itself to the existing layers that
Are anchored to the mountainside.

Sophie Gillanders (12)
South Molton Community College

STORM

As cold as ice
As wet as water
Like dry dust but cold wind
The rain coming down and people getting wet
Then the lightning strikes start and people running in.
Flash. Flash. Bang. Bang.
Pitter-patter
The storm is soon over
The wind is blowing.

Jason Meecham (13)
Tiverton High School

BROKEN HEART

Relationships are like a long
winding tunnel,
once you're in, you're stuck
until you decide to turn the next corner.
You feel all warm and excited inside,
you feel invincible, nothing can go wrong
until the sun goes in,
and the rain falls down.
He dumps you for her like a bag of rubbish,
you feel like your life is over.
You see them together wherever you go,
they smile,
you walk on,
no looking back,
you feel his eyes burning your back like a red-hot poker.
They are always hugging and kissing
in front of you,
as if to prove a point
but you get on with life.
You'll never heal your broken heart.

Jemma Sloman
Tiverton High School

SQUIRRELS

Like mad things jumping from tree to tree
on a psychotic search for anything worth eating.
Digging around through fallen leaves
for nuts and such like. Till the clump, clump, clump of
human feet and off up the tree again.

Rowan Grosse (13)
Tiverton High School

MY FIRST

First relationships are like driving down a long,
      winding country road, blindfolded.
They're a long roller-coaster ride which you control.
It's like being stung by a wasp, the shock goes on forever.
First relationships last as long as you make them.
Time is the last thing on your mind.
The shock is like diving into a pool of ice-cold water
And not knowing what to do, when you hit the water.
In first relationships you're free to do what you want to.
You can have fun. You can go out.
You'll do anything just to stay with him held in your arms forever.
You're obsessed, your books, everything covered with his name.
He's embarrassed.
But not all relationships last forever.
Mine didn't

Katie Hiscock (13)
Tiverton High School

My Safety Net

Oh, how I wish that there could be
A special library just for me.
A place to harbour all my thoughts
Where I could always steer to port.

This sanctuary would always hold
Coloured bottles appearing old.
Yet when the light would on them hit
My room with sparkles would be lit.

As those bright colours start to merge
The memories from my heart will surge.
On those walls my dreams will enact
Stealthily stolen from secret tracts.

Those magic photos seem so clear
They bring back all that I hold dear.
Soft laughter floating through the air
Music of which none can compare.

The bold aroma of childhood
Would forever linger onward
And if I closed my eyes so tight
I could conjure up marvels bright.

In these rainbows I will loiter
Till those visions start to falter.
When my light show concludes its case
Another race I'll boldly face.

Hannah Feerick (16)
Torquay Girls Grammar School

AIR RAID

Another drops down from the sky,
Thousands exploding all around,
Defences spilling sand feebly,
When will calm be found?

The people flee the stricken streets,
And underneath the park,
The lucky rest and shelter,
In the quiet and the dark.

Above the mayhem continues,
And a fiery thread is sewing,
All it took was a spark,
To get this fire going.

Metal and glass are flying,
As the bombs land from above,
War has ravaged London,
And destroyed the peace and love.

The wardens dodge the debris,
In a futile rescue attempt,
Of the many injured people,
From the bombs Hitler has sent.

The day dawns on an empty street,
And what horrors you see,
And this is only one bombing,
And how many more will there be?

All these years later,
The living remember the dead,
The War was one big funeral,
And for all wars the same can be said.

Bethany Ranjit (11)
Torquay Girls Grammar School

RAIN

Fast rain, slow rain
Everywhere you go rain
Drumming on the window pane
Falling on my brain.

Sometimes you get snow
And the flowers don't grow
And snowballs you can throw
And snowmen seem to grow.

Dry hair, wet hair
Raindrops getting everywhere
Over here, under there
Where you wouldn't dare.

Sometimes we see sleet
When we're eating Christmas meat
Lamplight glowing in the street
Children filled with Santa's treat.

Faye Willicott (14)
Whitstone Head School

TROLLEY FULL

I went to Sainsbury's on Thursday night.
The fruit and veg was a colourful sight.
The smell of the bakery filled the store
I loaded my trolley with more and more.

Seed for the budgie. Whiskas for the cat.
Bread and milk, I must not forget that.
I rush to the till. Join the queue.
I am amazed at the bill - *phew* ...
                    - *phew...*
                          -*phew!*

Sammy Davies   (12)
Woodlands School

EASY SHOPPING

I searched through the catalogue
to order my food.

Then I telephoned Iceland
in a good mood.

The lorry soon came with
all the goodies.

The shopping was easy
it saves my footies.

Richard Lee (12)
Woodlands School

THE BILL

I was paying for my food at the till
when I heard a *boom* what a thrill!

I was OO7 the agent from Devon.
My camera became a gun.
The till girl started to run
Towards me with her gun.
Rather than pay my bill
I shot to kill,
And set off all the *alarms*
                    alarms
                    alarms
                    alarms!

'Wake Up David!'

David Newby (11)
Woodlands School

FRUIT BURST!

I brought an orange one day.
It burst open on the floor.
I slipped and fell and said *'Hey!'*
I was frightened as well as sore.
I couldn't get up by myself,
So I grabbed at the packet drinks' shelf.
It came loose!
So much juice!

This was the worst,
Since my orange had burst!

Laura Body (12)
Woodlands School

SHOPOPHOBIA

The cupboards were bare - we needed some food.
We got in the van for Somerfield.
The shop
                full of trolleys
                bumping into each other.
Oh help! Let me out.

The shelves full of tins
                all making a din.
Oh help! Let me out.

The lemonade went pop
                quick get a mop
                I span in my chair.
Oh help! Let me out.

The trolley was full to the top of tins
                at last
I can get out!

Kerry Taylor (11)
Woodlands School

SHOPPING AT SAFEWAY

To the bus stop.
To the shop.

Me and Mum.

The 10 o'clock
For Tavistock
            Safeway is the store.

But we don't shop
The safe way
We spill things
On the floor.

Lemonade and orange juice,
Bananas in a bag,
The grapes all squashed
I hope they've washed
Their super shiny aisles.

Home by taxi
Cup of coffee
Me and Mum.

Rebecca Anne Hobbs (12)
Woodlands School